Living with the Aborigines

The experiences of a "little white fella" in Australia

Robert Westworth
(Robbie Cowboy)

ISBN-13: 978-1545291054

ISBN-10: 1545291055

Design & formatting by Socciones Editoria Digitale

www.kindle-publishing-service.co.uk

Contents

Chapter 1
Introduction

The temperature was in the high forties as the police patrol made its way along a dusty remote track in the central Australian outback. One of the officers yelled "Strewth look at that!"

Staggering towards them was a white man, dressed only in stubby shorts and a pair of sandals. He was covered from head to toe in a bright red rash.

As they drew near he dropped to his knees. His breathing was shallow and laboured. "Better get him inside." The two officers lifted him into the back seat of their Toyota personnel carrier. "Are you okay, what's wrong with you?" asked one of them. Having great difficulty breathing the man answered "I don't know".

"No time to get the flying doctor, he'll be a goner." Quickly they turned around and headed at full speed to the nearest aboriginal community with a medical centre - Indulkana. Twenty minutes later they pulled up in a cloud of dust, and after helping him up the front steps of the building the officer pressed the bell, got into the Toyota and drove off, leaving him shaking and doubled up on the platform.

There was no-one around. The medical centre was closed.

Who was this man, and what was he doing on a remote track in the Australian outback?

Here is the remarkable story of the Author, Robert (Robbie Cowboy) Westworth - and it all began way back in December 1937.

Chapter 2
The early days in England

I was born in December 1937 prematurely, weighing three and a half pounds, and was so small that my mother was scared to pick me up.

In those days there were no incubators, so I was wrapped in blankets and taken home by taxi. My grandmother kept me in a shoe box at the side of her bed making sure I was warm, and taking me into my mother for feeding at regular intervals. I was told that I was so small I didn't have the energy to cry.

My father was from an Irish family who came over to Liverpool at the time of the potato famine. They drifted down to Wolverhampton some time later, where my step grandfather found employment with LMS as a fitter in the railway sheds, maintaining coaches. His wife was a domestic help. The family originated in Knock, County Mayo, Northern Ireland, and in the early 1950s she went back to trace the family history - only to find that the wooden church had burned down, along with all the records of that time.

They lived in Thornley Street, Wolverhampton. My father was born in 1917, one of five siblings. His father, a kind and popular man, had a pawn shop in Peel Street. Unfortunately he died in 1918, in the deadly influenza pandemic which swept around the world. That pandemic killed between fifty and a hundred million people.

My father was also kind and quiet. He joined the army in 1939 and served until the end of the war. He worked hard, and became a regimental sergeant major. He passed away at the age of eighty four.

My mother's family came from Germany around the late 1800s. Her father was an engineer at a local steelworks, but decided to go into business on his own in 1940. He had a barber's shop at 156 Nechells Lane, Wednesfield, and mother did ladies hairdressing in the back. We also kept a couple of pigs, and grew our own vegetables, as was the norm at that time.

All the clients in my grandfather's shop were men whose employment varied from road sweepers to doctors. My mother's clients were women, and often while they were sitting waiting their turn, one would suddenly burst out crying. Mother would stop what she was doing, and the others would gather round the woman to comfort her.

In many cases a husband, boyfriend, or son, was missing in action or dead. My grandmother would then go into the kitchen to make her a cup of tea. That was a regular occurrence. Life was hard.

I'll never forget when I was three years old, standing on the front doorstep with my grandfather. We saw a red glow in the sky and suddenly heard a lot of muffled explosions. Grandfather spoke quietly and said "It looks like Coventry is having it bad." I didn't fully understand what was going on but I sensed it was bad. The Air Raid Wardens, or fire warden, would patrol the streets at night, and if anyone showed a chink of light he would shout at them to close their curtains or risk a fine. It was known that people were fined even if they were outside checking their blackout curtains.

There were no street lights or motor cars, people cycled everywhere. We could even distinguish between our aircraft and the enemy by their different sounds.

I remember also at that age, the sound of the air raid warning sirens. I was put under the stairs, beneath a stone slab in the pantry. I would stay there lying on a couple of small blankets, with my little Staffordshire bull terrier bitch Pat. There were no air raid shelters near us, so that was where we all stayed until the all clear was sounded. It's a funny thing, but as a little boy I became used to that way of life. There was no crying for toys - I accepted the fact that everything was in short supply.

Food was in short supply - everything was rationed. We had food coupons, sweet coupons and clothing coupons. Everything was 'make do and mend' with a saddle on my short trousers, and elbow patches on my jacket. Mother used to swap my sweet coupons for other coupons but it didn't bother me, that's how things were in those days.

I was walking to the park in Wednesfield one lovely sunny day and I sat down on a doorstep in Duke Street. I saw two men working on a cinder road near the park. One was Polish and the other was a blond haired blue eyed man named Kurt. They were both in about their early twenties, but seemed old to me. They were nice, and although I was only a child they sat and talked to me, and they told me all about their families back home.

A few days later they moved on. I told my grandfather and asked him why they had different material in the shape of a diamond sewn into their upper sleeves and the centre of their backs. "For the guards to shoot them if they run away" he replied. I was upset at the thought of my friends being treated that way.

One day one of grandfather's clients told us of how a scientist had gone up in a light aircraft from the airport (opened in 1938) that was adjacent to the Boulton and Paul factory. They discovered two radio waves crossing above Wolverhampton. That was how they managed to pin point night time bombing. The big guns were rushed to Wolverhampton for action, but a German spy must have warned the enemy and the raid was called off.

One afternoon I was in the garden when a twin engine plane passed so low he was almost at tree top level. He was trying to miss our village (Wednesfield.) In a doorway just behind the wing was a man wearing sandy brown overalls rippling in the wind. He looked as though he was undecided whether or not to jump, but the aircraft carried on heading for farmer Lewis's fields. There was a puff of black smoke and the engines stopped, followed by a loud crash. I ran into the house and told my mother. She put me in the child seat on the back of her Hercules push bike, and we headed across the fields to the crash site which was near to the Lichfield road and Lewis's bridge. The plane had hit overhead power lines and nose-dived into the field. Bits of aeroplane were scattered all around, and there was a strong smell of human flesh burning - it was a terrible scene.

We arrived before the police. Mother saw a man almost cut in two - he was still hanging on part of a wing. People were beginning to gather at the site, but it was all too much for my mother - she turned around and headed for home crying all the way, saying "That poor man." Seven crew members died in the disaster.

We had about a dozen laying Rhode Island red hens, and my job was to feed them and help in the garden by scraping butterfly eggs off the underside of the leaves of the cabbage plants. We had beds of onions, carrots, potatoes, gooseberry bushes, black currants, and an apple tree (cookers.)

All of that kept this little fella pretty busy. I had blonde hair, short back and sides, blue eyes, pale skin, and I was healthy and happy, although my

4

grandfather called me tin ribs due to my skinny build.

At the age of five I was taken daily to a kindergarten at a private house in Graisley Lane, Wednesfield. Sometimes my mother would take me and collect me in the afternoon, and sometimes my grandmother would take over. There I learned to tell the time, learnt the alphabet, and how to draw a cat sitting on a mat.

On our way back home we would stop at the paper shop to get a newspaper.

There were toys in the window - meccano sets and a beautiful yacht with its white sails and wooden deck.

I said once "Look at that nan, isn't it lovely?" and she replied "Yes, you can look at it but you can't have it because we can't afford it." That was ok with me. I understood, what with rationing and the war still in full swing. I was happy to stand and gaze in the window every time we passed the shop.

Whilst my father was away at war, my mother and I slept in the front bedroom above the barber's shop. One morning I was sitting on the edge of her bed while she was dressing me for kindergarten, and as usual I was fidgeting. Suddenly she gave me a hard slap to the face which almost knocked me off the bed. I sat up and stared at her through watering eyes, she was in a rage - why? She screamed at me "Keep still you little swine. If it hadn't been for you I wouldn't have had to marry him." With that she turned her back on me and sat down at her dressing table. I could see in the mirror tears running down her face. 'Oh mother why did you do that, I would never hurt you.' At that moment my happy little world was shattered, she might as well have killed me there and then. That episode drew me closer to my grandparents. From then on my relationship with mother was awkward and cold.

For many people the war seemed to drag on forever. I learned a lot by sitting in my grandfather's shop and listening to the conversation of his clients, mainly old men. I also learned to swear, much to their amusement and delight, 'bugger me' and 'bloody hell' would be met with roars of laughter.

Then one day the war was over. There was bunting in the streets of the village with lots of singing and dancing. Henry Meadows was a firm on the Cannock Road which made engines. They held a big party for all the children of their workers, and slowly the young men began returning home.

One day a man came to our house to stay. He was my dad! I didn't know who he was, and it was strange getting to know him.

Once again the road outside our house was alive with men going to work on pushbikes. The street lights were on at night. Some of my mother's clients were happy to get their men folk back, but unfortunately some were not so lucky. Eventually life began to settle down.

During the war we had Dolly, a Welsh pit pony, and trap. The old guy who looked after her would take me on short trips around Brewood or Essington.

I never told anyone what we did along with my lemonade and Frankie's beer swilling, but one day my grandfather took Dolly and me out for a ride, and then the penny dropped! At every pub we came to Dolly would stop and wouldn't move until she had her glass of beer. He saw the funny side of the situation and started to laugh saying "So that's what the old bugger's been getting up to."

Just before my ninth birthday the doctor was sent for. I had a raging sore throat and the glands in my neck were swollen. I had diphtheria and was rushed to Moxley isolation hospital. All my clothes and books had to be burned. With good treatment and nursing I survived, and was sent home in a taxi, bundled up in blankets.

As my grandfather carried me into the house a few snowflakes landed gently on my face. That was the beginning of the terrible 1947 winter, with the canals frozen solid for weeks along with snow drifts ten feet deep. I was confined to the house. Everything was so quiet, the road outside my bedroom was blocked with snowdrifts. It was a new and strange world to me.

The snow slipped off the roof at the rear of the house, completely blocking the door. Grandfather had to go out of the front door and dig his way round to the back. Even the shallow snow was about four feet deep. Eventually he dug out the rear door, but it left a tunnel like a fairytale landscape. The path to the chickens and pigs had to be cleared, but the next snow storm would cover up the paths again. It was a difficult time.

The canal behind the house where I would swim in the warm summer months was frozen to a depth of three feet. Some of the villagers had bonfire parties on the ice-bound canal. Children would be pushing an old cast iron bath up and down it and having a great time. The icebreaker gave up very soon as the ice thickened. This was a horse-towed shallow draught boat with eight or nine men rocking it furiously from side to side. None of the propeller powered boats made it through either.

It seemed strange - no roads filled with men on cycles going to or from work. Even the factories were unusually silent. There were no truck-mounted four-wheel-drive snow ploughs or gritting lorries in those days. The farms were hit hard, with many losing stock through cold and starvation. People also died. It seemed like ages before the paths were cleared and people could get to the shops.

When the weather did eventually change for the better, I was allowed to go back to the infant's school in Nechells Lane. During my illness I missed lessons which I would never catch up on - so by the time the 11 plus exams came around, I was losing interest in school activities. I would sooner be strolling in the countryside or swimming in some pond or canal. I moved on to Lichfield Road secondary modern school. All my results were good, but never-the-less I wanted to be free of the regimental type system, so when my grandparents purchased a small farm on the Shropshire Welsh border early in 1948 I jumped at the chance to go and live with them.

We moved to a stone cottage, Calcot cottage, situated half way up a mountain, above the small village of Priest Weston. After going through the traumas of the war it was pure heaven. The school I would be going to was about fourteen miles away in Welshpool. A bus would collect about sixteen children scattered around the local area and deposit us one hour later at school.

Every weekday morning I would leave home at seven fifteen and walk down to the village to a local family I knew. There I was given swede soup with a slice of bread (bread and soak) and a cup of tea before being picked up at eight o'clock by the bus driver.

They had a daughter who was the same age as myself and we were in the same class at school. She was a real tom boy. We would go for walks together and became good friends.

The school and its teachers were great, and I looked forward to attending each day. My whole outlook on life changed completely, my school reports were good and I was very happy.

The seasons were wonderful. Spring would bring the delightful scene of birds making nests and rearing their chicks - young rabbits running about the fields and mountains - lambs being born, and all the trees bursting into bud.

Summer and autumn were warm, making it pleasant for us to wander around the hills and valleys. Winter was like a Christmas card with the landscape covered in snow - icicles hanging down the small waterfalls like silver curtains touching the pools below, and stands of holly standing out in sharp contrast against the snow. The silence and solitude were calming and beautiful.

By the age of twelve I had learned the skills of a poacher. I would arm myself with a small American trenching shovel slung across my back, (as used by military forces, hikers, campers and other outdoor enthusiasts) - a penknife and a pocket full of purse nets, two small sacks tied around my knees with string and one over my shoulders. Then with my favourite ferret warm inside my shirt I would venture out into the snow. One foot deep was my limit finding rabbit tracks, and tracing them to their burrows where my ferret would do her work. Usually I would catch four or five rabbits. By that time I was glad to get home, put my ferret in her warm cage, and thaw myself out by the fire.

In summer life was much easier. I would cycle about three miles down to the river valley to check on my night lines for trout, and my eel traps. The river Camlad is the only river to run into Wales from England and back into England.

Five o'clock in the morning was the usual time for me to be down there. I wore an old poacher's jacket with one large pocket running all round the inside. By six o'clock it would be heavy and wet. I would sneak past the gamekeeper's cottage and watch for the signs of smoke coming out of his chimney. Thin blue smoke was okay - this meant he had just lit the fire and was about to boil the kettle for a cup of tea. Lots of smoke told me he had finished his cup of tea and was about to start his early morning patrol of the river with his shotgun and his hound. This meant that I would have to go back down to the river, wade across and climb a steep wooded slope to get to my bike which I had concealed behind a hedge in a farmer's field.

I would never sell my catch, it was always for my grandparents. That's why I wanted to be a part time poacher.

One Saturday morning I was late getting down to the valley to do my checking. There was a low mist covering the river, leaving me hidden below, but the old stone bridge was just above and the air was clear. Suddenly I heard footsteps. It was the gamekeeper. He came to a halt on the loose gravel on the centre of the bridge. Then there was silence. Everything went quiet except for the pounding of my heart.

At that moment I was about forty yards upstream from the bridge, standing quietly wondering what was going to happen next.

I didn't have to wait long - his old hound must have picked up my scent. He let out a loud howl that would have frightened the devil himself. He shouted "I know you're there." A shot rang out and a cluster of pellets hissed above my head as they tore their way through the cool damp morning air. It scared the hell out of me. I ran upstream, keeping low in the mist until I came to a bend in the river. No time to stop. I waded across, scrambled up a steep heavily wooded slope, eventually getting to my bike. When I got home I changed into dry clothes, then took a walk with my ferret tucked into my shirt and caught a couple of rabbits. I never told my grandparents what had happened.

I decided to keep away from the river for a while. In the meantime I found a couple of trout streams, but they weren't very productive, so I returned to my favourite spot on the river two weeks later, and I made sure I was always early - never late.

The journey to school was an adventure in itself, especially in the winter. There were days when I would battle through the snow to the village, only to find the bus couldn't get through to us. After breakfast we would go and play in the farm buildings for a short while. Then I would head back home, change into my old clothes and go ferreting, or gather wood for the fire.

Sometimes if the snow was coming down while we were at school, the headmaster would arrange for the bus company to pick us up early, at three o'clock, to make sure we were travelling home in daylight. The bus would often slide on the ice covered roads. The thaw also caused problems. The bus would sometimes have to go through water two feet deep or more, and water would flow inside the steps. I remember one day it was nudging floating telegraph poles with its front bumper. They had been stacked on the side of the road, but were floating dangerously in the road. When it got to be really bad we would take a detour through Leyton where the road was above the floodwaters of the river Severn. We were sometimes late for assembly, but due to our journey the school accepted this as the norm.

After getting home from school my first job was to go to the small fresh water spring which was about two hundred yards from the house. I had to carry two two-gallon galvanised buckets to bring back drinking water (it was lead free.) My next task was to hand-pump washing water from the stream which was twenty feet below the house (not lead free) to top up the storage tank behind the house.

After that my time was my own. It's a fact that although only twelve years old, I was mature beyond my years and happy with my life in the mountains.

In the winter when snow was on the ground, I would get my wooden ex-army sleigh from the shed, tie new ropes on it and drag it up over the fields at the back of the house to meet the grocery delivery man from Minsterly. He could go no further as the road was too steep and slippery. I would tie the provisions to the sleigh and struggle my way back down to the cottage and put the provisions inside. Then I would knock the snow off my sleigh, hang it back in the shed, and look forward to a nice hot cup of tea.

When my girlfriend and I were fourteen we became lovers. She was the same height as myself, slim, with dark curly hair, and well advanced for her years.

One hot summer day her mom, dad, two younger brothers and a younger sister went on a coach trip to Blackpool, leaving us to get ourselves off to school, but she had other ideas. At eight o'clock when the bus came to pick us up, we hid in a hayloft and watched as the bus drove off.

"Come on." She grabbed my hand and took me back to the house, and without another word she led me upstairs to her parents' bedroom. She closed the door, gave me an impish grin, and proceeded to pull her dress up over her head. She took off her knickers and stood there giggling. "Now it's your turn." She unbuttoned my shirt, took off my vest and pulled my pants down. Jumping on the bed she lay there teasing me. She pointed to the empty space beside her. "Come on" she ordered. I just stood there mesmerised by her beautiful naked body.

Eventually we dressed. We were kissing and hugging as we went down stairs. She cooked a dinner, then at about the same time as the school bus drove back through the village, I made my way home.

The following day neither of us spoke on the journey to school, or even in the classroom. The day seemed to drag, but going back home she came and sat next to me and held my hand. She gave me a big smile. "Do you want to see me tomorrow?" (that being Saturday.) Suddenly the dark cloud of gloom lifted and I felt happy and excited. "Yes, but it will have to be about twelve o'clock because I have a lot of wood to cut up in the morning."

She said she would meet me on the Miners Arms car park and we could have a walk up Llanfawr. That's a wild fern and gorse covered mountain. There was no chance of anybody discovering us, we could be alone and do whatever we wanted. "What about your mom and dad?" She began to smile. "Don't worry about them, although they don't show it they really like you."

On Saturday at mid-day I made my way down to the Miners Arms pub. My heart skipped a beat when I saw her in her pale summer frock - she looked pretty as a picture. I was fifteen minutes late. "Sorry for being late." She gave me a kiss and said not to worry, it was okay. It was one of those hot summer days - even the birds were keeping in the shade.

Her young brother and sister were playing nearby. "Where are you going?" "Just for a walk." "Can we come with you?" She frowned, "No you can't." "We want to come with you." "No." She took them both by the hand, walked them across the road, and slid them over a low stone wall into a field. "Now go and play."

11

They started to head for home and her brother looked back shouting angrily "I know what you two are up to, and so do mom and dad." It was a fact, they did, but they allowed us to continue our relationship and treated us as though nothing had happened.

We walked up the narrow track to the mountain gate. Passing through it seemed a different world - the ferns were taller than we were, and it was so quiet and peaceful. After about a ten minutes walk we came across a small hollow which was partly in the shade and partly in the sun. We were about sixty yards above a small mountain stream. The grass in the hollow was short and dry after being chewed by numerous sheep. It was a comfortable and private spot. Once again the girlfriend took control and we spent the time in each other's arms.

That evening when I got back to the cottage, I carried the drinking water from the spring as usual, and topped up the storage tank. Because it was a long summer evening I decided to go and check my rabbit traps - three rabbits had been snared. I gutted them and hung them in the wash house. We had no fridges in those days.

All the time I was checking the traps my mind kept wandering back to my girl that morning - then to her beautiful warm naked body when she lay on her parents' bed, and our love making. I lay awake most of the night, too excited to sleep.

On the Monday morning as I was on my way down to her house her father was walking towards me. He was a short muscular man with dark features and dark curly hair. He was stripped to the waist with a jacket slung over his shoulder. Normally he would smile and say "Hello young fella" but not this morning. He stood in the centre of the narrow road and threw his jacket to the ground. I said "Hello" and tried to walk to the left of his jacket, but he blocked my way. I tried to pass to the right but once again he blocked my path. I tried to force a smile but he was having none of it. "Get on that jacket" he ordered. "No I don't want to." "You might as well, you've been on everything else in the house." I froze on the spot - I didn't have a clue what he was talking about.

Picking up his jacket he gave me a stern look. "When you get to the house the missus wants a few words with you." With that he carried on his way. I thought I heard what sounded like a quiet chuckle, and as I watched him walk away I could swear I saw him shaking with silent laughter.

Walking into the kitchen the first thing I saw was my girlfriend sitting with her feet up on a bench and her chin resting on her knees, staring into the fire. She didn't even look at me. Her mother pulled out a chair and I sat at the table. She glared down at me. "Now mister bugger, I want a few words with you." There was a brief silence and I glanced quickly at her daughter but she was still staring into the fire. The mother continued to speak.

"Next time you get onto my bed take your bloody shoes off." She handed me my swede stew and I ate it quietly, not daring to look up. At last the school bus honked its horn, and we shot out of the house like a couple of scared rabbits.

One day we met by the old pit called the 'swallow' and she said she was going to show me something that would surprise me. We climbed over the boundary fence near an old track which led up to Corndon, and turning immediately left we climbed up a steep rock-covered slope to the top of the bank. "Where are we going?" I asked. "You'll see."

Walking through an old hawthorn hedge I saw that we were in a somewhat uneven field, but couldn't see anything unusual about it. "Are you playing games with me?" "No." She took my hand and led me towards the centre of the field. "Here we are."

At that point I was amazed to see the reason she had taken me there. It was a circle of fungi (mushrooms) around fifteen feet in diameter.

I had passed over that spot many times and never seen it - why? She took me into the centre and held me close to her.

"It's a fairy ring, can't you feel the magic?" "Yes I can." I felt an excited tingle as we stood there in an embrace in the circle. I loved her more than ever at that moment. Was it magic? I don't know - but it was a wonderful part of my young life.

It later dawned on me that I'd never spotted the fairy ring because I hadn't walked across the field during the mushroom season, a season that was very short there due to the altitude and cold weather.

As the day drew to a close we wandered back to her house where her mother gave us tea. "What have you two been up to?" She just smiled and said "Not a lot mom."

During the whole of 1951and 1952 we made love as often as possible. We would go to her bedroom and get into bed like a married couple. Life was wonderful - but time moves on.

The beginning of 1953 found me working in my first job as a farm hand on a two hundred acre farm - Rorrington Hall - part of the Sir Olfley Wakeman estate, earning one pound a week. She worked in domestic service in a big house near Whitchurch. We lost touch with each other but I never forgot our wonderful time together.

My early morning tasks as a farm hand were that I would help the head cowman with milking, then go on to ploughing - or sowing corn, potatoes or swedes. In the summer I helped with the harvest, and in the sheep shearing season I helped to pack the fleeces into large wool sacks. At lambing time I would help with the birth of the lambs, and if cows were calving I would be involved. There were also hedges and ditches to be maintained. What you might call general farm work. In my second year on the farm I had a wage rise, bringing it to one pound and ten shillings.

The servants' room was in Rorrington Lodge which was approximately two hundred yards to the rear of the Hall, situated at the top of a small hill. It stood in its own grounds, and was a large imposing brick building with turrets. There was a tennis court and a cockpit which was accessed by a small wicket gate into a nearby field, and a number of outbuildings.

Whilst working on the farm winters could be quite severe, with snow drifting off the fields onto the narrow road, making it impossible for me to make the three miles uphill trip back home. On these occasions I would have my evening meal and sleep at the Lodge which was tenanted by the farmer's son and his wife. After the meal I would go to my bedroom up a spiral stone staircase. My single mattress was stuffed with straw, a bit uncomfortable at first, but I soon became used to it and had some good nights' sleep. I would also have my breakfast at the Lodge.

One evening on my way to bed I had to pass through a short hallway. To my right was a glass display cabinet which contained three shelves and stood about four feet high. On each shelf were figures about ten inches high standing on round wooden bases. They were Indian warriors standing smartly to attention with turban head dresses and holding spears. On each base were the words 'Presented to Robert Clive.' I only knew of one Robert Clive, he was Clive of India, Sir Robert Clive.

Lunch would be at the Hall with the tenant farmer and his wife. This was served on a long oak table in the servants' quarters. There were about five or six bells hanging on the wall above our heads. It was a large black and white, half timbered building. I went into some of the rooms. There was one I remember with oak panelling.

There were five full time staff working at the Hall. The farmer and his wife were the only people living there. They were in their mid sixties. She did the cooking and was a lovely woman, she always gave me plenty of food. I think the place has been taken over now by some posh dining establishment.

As a young man, working on the farm had a couple of bonuses, one of which was a trout stream running near the house, round the rear of the cattle sheds and on through the fields. On my time off I would go and tickle a few trout, a skill taught to me by one of the farm workers. Sometimes there would be a nest of wild bees with their homes in rabbit holes. With the aid of a handful of dried grass and a match I would smoke them out and help myself to some of the honey, but I would never destroy the hive. I also became pretty good at catching pheasants. I would never take as much as a turnip from the farm or a bale of straw, because the farmer had told me "If you want anything boy, ask and I will give it to you, never steal." I respected him for this.

In the May of my third year I had a serious motor cycle accident which left me with a broken tibia and fibula four inches above the ankle of my right leg. It was protruding through the skin. Also, due to a head injury I drifted in and out of consciousness for three days, and it took six months altogether for me to recover.

The hospital was in the centre of Shrewsbury, the Royal Salop Infirmary I think it was called. I was in Men's surgical B, at the rear of the ward on a glass bottomed balcony exposed to the weather. When it rained the nurses would drape a rubber cover over my bed. There was another man on the same balcony. There were more balconies at the rear of the building overlooking the river Severn and the football field. I think it was called gay meadow.

The three weeks I was in there are somewhat clouded due to my head injury, but I do remember the surgeon who operated on me twice - and his assistant. I also remember that the matron was strict, no one argued with her! One happy recollection is that of the barber who used to shave us with a shaking hand and whiskey breath. He fell down the steps at the front of the building and ended up in the ward with a broken leg - served the drunken old bastard right. He used to put the fear of god up me when he was shaving me.

My next move was to Gobowen Rehabilitation Centre in Oswestry. I was there for about two months, after which I was well enough to be discharged. I returned to work on the farm, but the wages were so poor that I found it necessary to move on, and decided to enter the construction industry.

In 1958 my grandparents moved back to their old property in Wednesfield and I moved with them. Times were difficult, and I decided to move into lodgings with a local Italian family. There were three brothers and two sisters. Katrina (Cathie) was one year younger than myself. She was beautiful and I was drawn to her by her big hazel eyes. In less than a year we were married.

The next seven years found me working in the motor trade on the engineering side, but in 1966 I decided to establish my own business in the haulage industry.

The business, Westworth Haulage, was registered at my home 46 Mill Lane, Wednesfield.

After ten years there was general unemployment. This affected my business badly and the future looked bleak. I was having trouble getting money from my main contractor which left me late paying my tax bill (the first time in ten years.) The woman in the tax office in Wolverhampton was a real snotty bitch. All I asked for was time to pay. "If you don't pay we'll commandeer your wife's car." It was in my name. I returned home and told Cathie what had happened. That was the final straw, so we decided to emigrate and start a new life in Australia. Cathie's sister and her family had emigrated there in 1975.

Chapter 3
Beginning life in Oz

We took an assisted passage costing around £100 each. The journey took twenty six hours on a Quantas Airlines Jumbo 747, arriving in Melbourne in January 1977.

We found a home in the suburbs, Mooroolbark and three months later we were joined by our two Staffordshire bull terriers, Tanya and Togo, on their release from quarantine. Once we were established we made good Australian friends, both white and aboriginal.

Things went drastically wrong two weeks after arriving. Cathie received the bad news that her father had died, and she was devastated at not being able to go back for the funeral and to see her mother. We had put a large deposit on the house and purchased a car which meant that our funds had run out. We had also lost out on the exchange rate, it was quite a shock but I didn't let the grass grow under my feet. I got a job at Kenworth Trucks Propriety Limited, Bayswater 3153.

However I didn't relish the idea of emigrating to Australia only to end up in a large factory, therefore I would keep scanning the Melbourne Age newspaper until something better came along. It did - and I commenced employment on 14th August 1978 with Blackwood Hodge, Victoria 3175, in the capacity of demo operator and installation engineer.

Their heavy construction equipment consisted of JCB backhoe front-end loaders, Terex twin power scrapers, dozers, front end loaders, Timberjack log skidders, mobile cranes both on tracks and truck mounted to eighty tons, and O&K face shovels.

Often I would pack my overnight bag and be away from home for a week or more, and my travels took me into the outback of South Australia, all of the state of Victoria, parts of New South Wales and Tasmania. I was in my element! Anything from gold mines in Balarat to kaolin pits in Victoria, talcum quarries in South Australia, forests in the central highlands of

Tasmania, all the local shires in Victoria and the Loyang Power Station.

I could be compared to a gypsy always travelling, the only difference being that instead of a caravan my overnight stays were in motels, hotels, and sometimes pubs. I was more like a well-groomed Romany, but I enjoyed my job.

I had to take one of the salesmen on a courtesy visit to a small privately run gold mine just over the New South Wales border. We drove to a remote area covered in sand dunes, and eventually arrived in a clearing where there was a wooden hut with one side missing. In it was a fridge, a couple of chairs and a table. Round the back was a small generator servicing the fridge and a couple of light bulbs. About twenty feet away was an open top tank about eight feet long, four feet wide, and about six feet high, containing acid as part of the gold mining process. There didn't seem to be anyone there, but after a few minutes two Jed Clampit look-alikes appeared.

They were tall with weather-beaten faces, wearing bib and brace overalls. They looked too old to be doing this job, but appearances can be deceptive. They were both millionaires and really nice blokes. They knew the salesman from past deals and were happy to see him. They shook us by the hand, almost breaking my fingers. After talking business they offered us a mug of tea and a sandwich. I declined the sandwich after spotting their stew pot with a thick lining of fur around its inner edges, but I didn't say anything to the salesman.

One of the men opened the fridge and took out a loaf and some butter and cheese. "Bloody blow flies" he said, reaching for the fly spray and spraying it wildly in the air. It did the trick, but some of the blowies were falling onto the buttered bread. Not to worry though, he brushed them off with his hand. I watched as the colour began to drain from the salesman's face as somewhat reluctantly he picked up his sandwich and began to eat it. He couldn't refuse, after all he was there to make a sale. That's what I call dedication to the job!

"We'll have to go now, come on Bob." He got into the car quickly and I noticed he was beginning to turn green. After driving a short distance and out of sight of the men he screamed "Stop the car." Before it stopped he was out and giving it the technicolour yawn. It took nearly seven hours to reach Melbourne and I thought he was dead, he'd been so quiet, but he managed to drag himself to his car and drive off.

I was requested to go to Tasmania another time for a week, to instruct grader drivers on two new Canadian graders, supplied by the Blackwood Hodge depot in Tasmania. I flew out from Melbourne in a Focker Friendship turbo-prop non pressurised aircraft. On the way we encountered a hail storm and it sounded as though someone was throwing stones onto a caravan roof, it was deafening. "What a start" I thought to myself.

Not to worry, we arrived safely in Davenport where I was met by the Blackwood Hodge manager - a tall smartly dressed man in his early fifties with short cropped blonde hair and a grin from ear to ear.

"Hello Bob, we'll be spending a week in the central highlands grading forestry roads, and I want you to look at some Terex bulldozers and front-end loaders in a quarry. I suspect the men aren't operating the equipment correctly and are causing us a few problems." As we headed towards his car he asked the sixty four thousand dollar question "Do you drink?" I hesitated "Occasionally" I replied. "Are you a social drinker?" "Sort of." "Good." With that we got into his car and headed for the Blackwood Hodge depot. Little did I know what I was letting myself in for.

The first day we had a transmission problem with one of the machines as it was being prepared in the workshop, but thanks to a few contacts I was able to help them sort it out.

That night after tea I went with a couple of the staff, including the manager, for a few Bacardi and cokes in the bar of the motel. They were quite nice and I began to get a taste for them. When the bar closed we went to the rooms where we were booked in and drank the mini bars dry and all the drinks in the fridges. First one room, then another, then another, and then on to mine (no pressure.)

The next day we took the graders on low loaders into the central highlands where I began instructing the operators on how to get the best out of their machines. We ended up in a place called Queenstown and covered a few miles before returning to the motel for our evening meals. Then to the bar and the mini bars in the bed rooms. I was beginning to like this set up. This routine continued for the rest of the week and my visit was a success, in as much that everything I was sent to do was achieved.

Just before I boarded the Tri Star in Launceston for my one hour flight back to Melbourne the manager shook my hand and thanked me for my help, and added that he would be sending a fax to the Melbourne depot thanking them too.

As I sat in my seat the nightly flow of Bacardi and coke caught up with me. "Will passengers fasten their safety belts?" Okay, I clicked it shut. "Will passengers fasten their safety belts?" I checked and it was already fastened, BUT we were coming in to land at Tullamarine airport in Melbourne. Turned out I had passed out after fastening the belt for take-off and had slept like a baby (not a very good looking one) with a giant hangover for the rest of the flight.

As I wobbled out of the aircraft into the airport Cathie and a couple of friends were there to drive me home. She took one look at me. "You look ill, are you okay?" "Yes I'm okay." "Are you sure?" "Yes love, it's a long story, I'll tell you later."

Our first house was a single storey on a large corner plot, and at the rear was a patio partly in the shade which was welcome during the hot summer months. We had a round wooden garden table on it with two benches. The garden sloped steadily downhill, and at the back of our boundary the ground rose gently for about three hundred yards. At the top stood a big old gum tree within easy sight of the house and there was nest of magpies in the tree. They were almost as big as a domestic hen and had a fearsome reputation for swooping at people if they went near the nest. The old cock used to fly past and he soon came to realize that the bits of bread Cathie was putting on the table were for him.

After a day or two he was joined by his hen which also enjoyed the meal. Gradually they became used to our presence and our dogs Togo and Tania. The cock would stand on the table and sing his heart out - it sounded like someone playing a flute. Even the dogs just lay on the benches and seemed content to listen to him. They didn't move even though he was only a couple of feet away from them.

It was a wonderful sight as the pair glided silently from their nest down to the house with hardly a wing beat. If Cathie was late putting out the bread the cock would peck on the kitchen window as if to say "Come on Cathie." One day instead of two magpies gliding down there were four. They'd brought their two chicks to introduce them to us and they were almost as big as the two old ones. After having their feed the chicks would play in the branches of a small tree near the patio, swinging about and play fighting, they would then perch in the lower branches maybe two feet off the ground and fall fast asleep.

Our dog Tania was going to walk down the garden and Cathie said "Don't wake the magpies." It was as though she knew and walked slowly and quietly past them. The magpies seemed to be making us their second home.

One hot dusty morning tragedy struck in the most cruel of circumstances. After they had been fed the cock and hen flew off, leaving the chicks playing as usual around their favourite tree. I watched them as they flew a short distance away and flying near a tall pole which was carrying two high voltage cables. As they flew around the top there was a loud crack and they both dropped onto the road below. Horror stricken I rushed to the pole only to find one chick with blood coming out of his beak - it was obvious he'd broken his neck and was dead. The other one was lying face down with his wings spread out. Very gently I closed his wings and held his head straight as I slid him into my shirt.

As I stepped onto the patio Cathie was waiting for me, not knowing what had happened. She burst into tears as she saw the unconscious bundle of feathers I was holding to my chest.

She cried even more when I told her what had happened and that the other chick was dead. I realized my vision was becoming blurred - I too was crying.

I held the chick keeping his head steady and praying that he would keep breathing. After about five minutes he stirred. I knelt down and held him in my cupped hands, I didn't want to risk him falling to the floor. 'Don't die chick, please don't die.' He began to look around and seemed confused. At first he was hesitant, then he took off and headed for the safety of the gum tree.

We were both still crying while we buried the poor dead chick near the small tree which they used to play in and have so much fun. The cock and hen and their surviving chick never returned, and Cathie and I were devastated.

For two weeks each year I instructed and carried out government certification on would-be operators at the School of Mines and Industries, Ballarat 3350 Victoria. The weather was hot, but after work the beer was cool. I was beginning to like Australia! I remained with the company for three years.

I got talking to one of the Shire engineers one day near Bendigo. He worked for the local council in their depot where they stored their graders and road making equipment. It was mid-day, the weather was hot, and I was looking forward to a nice cold beer.

As we chatted I saw something fall out of a nearby hedgerow and as it hit the ground it created a cloud of dust. "What the hell was that?" Walking over to the spot I picked up a parrot. "Poor thing, it's dead." The engineer took a close look at it and began to laugh. "No it's not dead, it's drunk." There weren't any beer barrels or bottles around so how could the bird be drunk?

He pointed to the big old hawthorn hedge that ran along the top of the yard. "It happens pretty often. You see those hawthorn berries, well they get full of them, they ferment in their gut and they end up drunk. You've heard the saying 'as pissed as a parrot' well now you know why. Oh and by the way, put it in the shade somewhere away from the cats and he'll recover."

That brings me to another little story concerning drunken birds (feathered types.) Cathie and I were in our back garden one day. It was beautifully warm and the birds were busy catching insects. As she walked along the patio she discovered a small honey eater bird lying on the floor. "Poor little thing, look at this Bob." She handed the small bundle of feathers to me and it began to stir, moving its head shakily from side to side. It appeared to vomit and a tiny drop of liquid came out of the long slim beak into my hand.

We had never seen anything like this before. Suddenly the head shaking became more vigorous and I felt the wings and legs move. It looked around like a drunken man. Then I opened my hands and it flew away. Cathie began to laugh. "Would you believe it Bob that bird was drunk, now I've seen everything." With that we sat on the patio and had a nice cool beer. If the honey eaters could do it so could we!

The house backed on to farmland which was quiet and peaceful, but two days after we moved in rock blasting began for sewer pipes to be laid and homes to be built on the farmland.

We decided then that as soon as we were financially sound we would move into the mountains, but we had made many friends and had lots of barbeques - life was good.

Quite often when working for Blackwood Hodge I would drive heavy mobile cranes between their Melbourne, Adelaide and Sydney depots, in order for customer inspection and trials. On one such occasion I took a forty ton crane to Adelaide from our depot in Melbourne. The route through Melbourne city was a designated one which we had to stay on until we were clear of the city limits.

Once we were on the main highways the restrictions didn't apply. All we had to adhere to were the speed limits through small towns en route, but it was a long job taking all day. The weather was hot and dusty but there was no time to pull over for refreshments.

As I approached the river Murry it turned out the crane was too heavy for the newly constructed road bridge spanning the river. Luckily my documents directed me away from the bridge, first to Tailem bend then follow the sign for the Jerviouse ferry. If it was too big for the bridge I was praying it wouldn't be too big for the ferry. As I neared the ferry two cars were waiting ahead of me and it was already in position to take on cargo. As I parked up and applied the air brakes a worried looking ferry master walked over and inspected the crane.

He scratched his head and said "I'll have to take you on your own." He ushered the waiting cars to one side then signalled me to drive behind him. "If her nose dips when you get the front axles on, for Christ's sake don't stop, keep her going and keep tight in to the wheel house." This remark didn't fill me with confidence, but I did as he said - and yes, the ferry dipped almost under water as the two steer axles mounted the deck, but I kept her going and somewhat shakily I parked her tight against the wheelhouse. "Don't get out, stay in the cab." "Okay." After a fair amount of swaying we reached the concrete apron on the other side of the river, and after making the ferry secure the captain stood on the road and signalled me to come forward.

I could see the tension in his face. "Come on, keep her going." Slowly I drove off and once again it dipped, its nose almost under water as I went up the incline away from the river. He gave me a wave, and the look on his face was one of relief - so was mine.

As I approached the outskirts of Adelaide it was beginning to get dark and the descent into Adelaide was down a long, steep and dangerous hill. I parked up at the top, the Eagle on the Hill Hotel, to use their pay phone to get a member of Blackwood Hodge staff to guide me through Adelaide to their depot in Port Augusta - and a well deserved beer. As I went to check

24

that the crane was locked a dusty old Ford ute parked up alongside me. In the back of it were about six men all wielding base ball bats. 'Must be some sort of trouble' I thought, 'better get back into the bar.'

About twenty minutes later a young mechanic came and found me in the bar. He looked worried. "You can't go down the hill, there's a truckies' strike on." Seemed that while I was making my way to Adelaide, somewhere on the outskirts of Sydney a truckie with his CB call sign 'yellow dog' had called a national strike and everyone had followed suit. "If you like I can take you on a back road into and through Adelaide." I wasn't impressed with this statement. There was a designated route through Adelaide and there was no way I was going to ignore this paperwork. I asked him out of curiosity "Is it a narrow road?" "Yes." "Okay you say it's narrow, will it take this forty ton crane?" He frowned, "I don't know."

I walked over to the crane taking my overnight bag out. "Here are the keys. Can you take me to a motel, I have to catch a flight back to Melbourne in the morning. The crane stays here until your office sorts something out."

As we drove down the Eagle on the Hill the highway was crammed with parked trucks. We had a job to squeeze through with a car. Good job I parked up at the top, there were some pretty wild truckies marching around with pick shaft handles. I would have hated to upset any of them. Once in the motel I had a shower and an evening meal, and the next morning I caught my ten o'clock flight. Not long after that the truckies' strike was over.

It was mid-summer when for one week a Sales team from Blackwood Hodge Melbourne and another team from Sydney, about ten men in all, descended on the small timber and tobacco growing town of Myrtleford.

Myrtleford consisted of heavily timbered rolling hills, a valley and flat area, with a beautiful shallow river which nudged its way over a bed of polished pebbles.

It was the Forestry Industries Mechanical Exhibition (FIME.) We had Timberjack logging equipment, Dremco graders, Manitou forklifts and a Terrex bull dozer on display. There were also other Sales teams and Companies from Melbourne attending the exhibition, it was very busy.

Everything went well on the first day - that was until the evening. The first disaster was our team from Melbourne running out of cash in the pub.

There was total panic, but after some hard bargaining we got the Sales team and their Management from Sydney to pay the bill for the rest of the evening's grog.

The next disaster occurred much later into the evening. It was the worst imaginable. Big tough men were reduced to tears. The pub ran out of beer - yes we drank the pub dry. Next to earthquakes and landslides this was classed as a major disaster. The next day was terrible. Everyone drank water and tea (no grog) but glory be, the pub saved the day by getting an emergency supply of beer delivered from Melbourne the very next day. We had to go steady though for the rest of the week due to the restricted cash flow.

Whilst I was there I did some wandering around the area in my spare time. The low banks of the river were covered in what looked like butterflies flitting onto the surface of the slow running river and back onto the bank. Their colours were varied and spectacular. It turned out they weren't butterflies at all but very small birds similar to a wren.

There were low thatch covered sheds with open sides and widely spaced inner framed wooden racks about three feet off the floor. They were tobacco drying sheds. All in all it was a truly beautiful and interesting area. The week passed quickly and it had been a great success for Blackwood Hodge regarding sales, marred only by the terrible disaster of that first night in the pub.

A couple of weeks later I took Cathie up there to see the area around Myrtleford. She loved it and at lunch time we had a beer and a meal in the pub. It was much quieter that day and the beer was cool - totally different from when the men were crying into their empty glasses. I love Australian pubs, so much goes on there and you meet some interesting characters (great stuff.)

I travelled to an aboriginal reserve at Nowa Nowa in the eastern part of Victoria to install and instruct on two new graders supplied to them by Blackwood Hodge. I was there for a couple of days. It was the first time I had met any of the local aborigines, and I found they were great guys. I clicked with them right away and was really happy with their attitude towards this little pommie white fella. I must admit I felt totally at home with them.

They were very adaptable when it came to operating the graders and I was impressed by the fact that they had a great sense of survival and wouldn't take unnecessary risks when it came to the safety of themselves and the machines, i.e not travelling on dangerous side slopes where the machine could slip or tip over sideways. Soon it was time for me to leave and travel back to Melbourne.

I was approaching a small town called Traralgon. When I got to about half an hour's drive from there I spotted what looked like a bundle of clothes in the deep grass to the left of the highway near a parked car. As I got closer I saw that it was a man. It looked as though he had passed out. Parking behind his car I went quickly over to him and found him crumpled up and unconscious.

I checked his airway, it was clear, he was breathing okay, no signs of blood or vomit. I checked the bottom of his legs for signs of snake teeth marks, there weren't any, his limbs felt okay as far as I could tell. Not being a doctor I was relying on my first aid training. 'Better put him in the recovery position and try to hold his head in a comfortable position - what the hell am I going to do now?'

In those days there were no cell phones, I had no radio communication equipment, the vehicle wasn't set up for it. The highway in those days was a single carriageway, (today it's a dual highway) and to make matters worse the road was quiet, but there was no way I was going to leave the man.

Luckily after about twenty minutes a car drew to a halt near us and a woman maybe in her thirties got out and came to my aid. She checked the man over in what seemed a very professional manner and as she did so I saw a car approaching headed for Traralgon. I flagged him down and asked him to call in at Traralgon and get an ambulance to come for the man. He sped off but I still had to stay with the unconscious man and the woman.

After what seemed like ages I heard the siren of the ambulance. Before it got within sight the woman headed for her car. "Aren't you going to wait for the ambulance?" "No, you hold his head steady until they get here. I'm a nurse and if anything happens to this man the family could sue me." I was surprised at that statement, but it was true - there was a suing culture in Australia in those days.

Anyway the ambulance arrived, turned around, and took the still unconscious man to hospital. I carried on my way to Melbourne knowing I had done what I could for him, and I hoped that someone would do the same for me if I were in that position. I'm sure they would.

Travel to my demos and plant installations in Victoria usually took a day to get there and a day to get back when going by road. Then I could be on site for two or three days, meaning that most weeks Cathie wouldn't see me until the weekend.

Sometimes I would fly out and back, that was much easier and quicker. One particular day I travelled to the small coastal town of Aries Inlet. It was beautiful with its many small inlets and low hills sweeping into the sea.

The small Plant Hire Company had received two new JCB front end loader backhoes, and after the operator instruction was completed I carried on instructing the mechanics on the servicing of the machines. When I had finished the boss was pleased with my work with the men, so much so that he invited me to his home for a meal and a drink.

The only way to his home was over a narrow bridge over a tidal inlet. As I approached the bridge I noticed a rowing boat moored up, and perched along one side were three well fed pelicans enjoying the warm sunshine. His home was built snugly into the side of a hill one hundred yards further on.

After the meal and a pleasant couple of beers he took me to one side. "You did a good job there, how would you like to work for me? I'll pay you double your wages, and you'll have good prospects for the future. You'll be better off than working for a multi-national company." I didn't make rash decisions, so I thanked him for his offer and said that I would have to talk it over with Cathie first.

Soon it was time for me to head back to Melbourne. As I passed over the narrow bridge the tide was coming in and the rowing boat which then had five pelicans perched along its side was swirling about on its mooring and tilted sideways at a steep angle. Thinking no more about it I carried on making my way home. The next day I discussed his offer with Cathie but she wasn't happy with the idea of moving at such short notice - plus I was happy at Blackwood Hodge.

That evening I phoned him and told him what we'd decided. He was disappointed but agreed that it was our decision to make. During the conversation I mentioned the five pelicans on the rowing boat and he began to laugh. He told me that nine pelicans had eventually perched along the side and their combined weight caused the boat to dip beneath water level. They stayed perched on it until it sank and then calmly swam away without even ruffling a feather!

With that he wished me luck and said goodbye. So there it was - I'd been offered a good job on the coast, and learned that pelicans can sink a rowing boat!

A lot of people I speak to think the capital of Australia is Sydney but it isn't. It is in fact the land-locked city of Canberra A.C.T. (Australian Capital Territory.) It was one place I had always wanted to visit, so you can imagine my excitement when one Friday morning I was called into the Area Manager's office. He was a tall well built man in his early fifties with short cropped blonde hair. He always wore smart trousers with creases you could cut your fingers on, a light shirt, slim tie, and a blazer.

He was sitting at his highly polished roll topped desk. "Sit down Bob, I want you to go to Canberra on Monday for a week, and install two new JCB front end loader backhoes. Your hotel is booked and you can pick up your tickets at the Reg Anset booking desk at Tullamarine airport first thing Monday morning." I left his office with a smile on my face from ear to ear.

When I got home the first thing I did was to pack my overnight bag until it bulged. Cathie was great, she never moaned when I went away. Maybe she was glad of some peace and quiet! She dropped me off at the airport on Monday morning and kissed me goodbye. Even though I was excited I never liked leaving her, but a man must do what a man must do.

My seat was one away from a left hand window. "Excuse me." A young woman squeezed past into the seat next to me and we got talking. It turned out she was on her second ever flight and was nervous. Not to worry, she was going to see her boyfriend and visit Canberra at the same time. We settled down for the short flight and soon we were approaching Canberra airfield. The descent was over low hills which caused turbulence, and it was rough to say the least. The aircraft was shaking and rattling, and it felt like sliding down a set of stairs on a tea tray.

The girl was terrified. She grabbed my hand and began to squeeze my fingers almost breaking them, but I didn't pull away. If it helped her then I would let her get on with it. She didn't let go until we had taxied to a stop, and her relief was obvious. Looking down at my fingers they had turned white with the lack of blood flow, but the main thing was that she was okay - and the feeling and colour soon returned.

I collected my bag and found my hotel. After booking in, I phoned the customer and arranged to be taken to the transport depot where the two machines were waiting.

We then took them out to where they would be working. They were digging a gas pipeline through Canberra. At that point there were no gas services, and if anyone bought an electric cooker or washing machine, or other household goods, there was a Border Tax when it entered the A.C.T. It sounded a bit expensive to me. Anyway the job went well, and every night the lads would take me to sample a few beers in different pubs and hotels.

One afternoon I found myself with time to kill, so I visited the museum where a Japanese mini sub was standing on a concrete plinth. Someone said it had been sunk in Sydney Harbour during the last war. Leading away from this was a wide highway, and at the top were the parliament buildings - very impressive. Then I wandered near a large lake where I saw a tall square sided structure. I was told it was a musical instrument and there was only one woman who could play the thing, but she wasn't there that day.

The night time visits to sample the grog carried on right up to the time I caught my flight back to Melbourne, and by the time Cathie picked me up at the airport I had a giant hangover. She couldn't understand why I was so quiet, but I think she had a good idea just what I'd been up to. Thus ended my visit to Canberra.

After my three years at Blackwood Hodge I moved on to Ascom Equipment, Nantila Road, Clayton. They manufactured and installed electricity pylons and grain silos. They had a few fatalities, with men falling from pylons. Some of their crane drivers weren't fully skilled, and this caused problems between the company and the authorities. Also their insurance costs were going up. Therefore the job of Training Officer was created. My job was to visit all construction camps, observe and advise operators in the safe use of equipment - mobile winches, mobile cranes, tower cranes, drilling rigs, diggers and other plant, re-train rusty operators and certifty them to the standard required by the Department of Labor and Industry.

Once again I was travelling throughout the state of Victoria and South Australia, but instead of staying in motels and hotels, I reserved a room on whichever construction site I visited and ate with the men, mainly Italian.

I would sometimes start out at three o'clock in the morning in order to get to the construction camp for seven thirty and have breakfast with men. There I would organise my day travelling down the power lines under construction to check if the men had any problems with the machines.

One morning at about five o'clock I was travelling on a narrow road in the west of Victoria. There were deep ditches on either side of the road, and as I approached a narrow T-junction I spotted something very odd.

A black ute (pick-up truck) was parked about twenty yards facing the junction to my right. White exhaust smoke was surrounding the rear of the vehicle. As I neared the intersection standing in the centre of the road was a wine flagon which had I tried to avoid meant that I would've ended up in the ditch on one side or the other.

The driver of the ute was revving up its engine in the stationary position and it was obvious what was going to happen. Nothing for it but to give my old Ford Falcon full throttle, and aim full centre at the flagon. By then I was doing about a hundred and fifty kilometres per hour and still accelerating. I hit it dead centre with the bumper. All I heard was a thud. The ute must have been a V8 - as I looked in my mirror it swung into view. "Come on old girl, you can do it." All I could see were two shapes in the cab. Gradually I lost them, but I still kept my foot down.

I have to admit I was shaken. If I had been unfortunate enough to hit the flagon with a tyre I would have lost control and ended up in the ditch, and I've not the slightest doubt that I would have been robbed and possible murdered.

When I got to the camp I was glad to have a black coffee laced with grappa to settle me down. What did I do about it? Nothing. I just put it down to luck that I was okay.

I would pack an overnight bag on Sunday evening, and Cathie wouldn't see me again until the following Friday evening. A company car was provided and a good yearly bonus was added to my wage. Slowly the men became more safety-minded and my presence was more appreciated by them. I learned some Italian from the various line foremen, but this was mainly swearing!

We had lots of Australian University students visiting the camps, and on one occasion an old foreman told me that he had almost fallen down the ladder of a tower crane when a young female student told him she had learned to say "Good morning" in Italian "Va afen coolo." I wouldn't repeat that in English!

Whilst I was working at Ascom we moved into the mountains. Our home was on the lower slopes of Mount Donnabuang with the river Yarra below. Every July and August the snowline would end two hundred yards above the house, and the deer would come down for the mosses and lichens. Cathie would take our dogs for walks down along the river. The area around the small village of Warburton was nick-named 'little Switzerland' and during the weekends I would sit on the balcony at the back of the house and enjoy the view of the valley and hills.

Sometimes flocks of black cockatoos would fly along the valley and it seemed strange to be looking down at the tops of their wings as they passed. It was all so peaceful. In the winter we would drive down to Warburton, and go up along the mountain road to the snow at the top of Mount Donnabuang. Sometimes the lyre birds with their delicate tails which looked as though they were made of black lace would dart across the snow covered road. Everything was beautiful.

Work for Cathie was hard to find early on, but as time progressed she was able to get employment as a teacher's aide in a small school in Powel town surrounded by forestry land. It was heaven - she loved every minute there. She also got involved in a postal art course.

My job with Ascom was very successful, so much so that I was beginning to get bored and unsettled. So I began my search for more challenging employment and travel. This came in the form of a vacancy with a gold mining company in Papua, New Guinea. My interview was successful and I was given the position of Technical Training Officer with OK Tedi Mining Limited - so I was soon on my way to new climes.

Chapter 4
Gold Mining in Papua New Guinea

It took Cathie an hour to drive me from our home to Tullamarine airport in Melbourne. Saying goodbye to her was always difficult, I loved her so much, but she knew that this was the only way for me to put some decent money into our bank account. Office and factory work were out of the question, I just couldn't hack it - no way.

The first flight was to Sydney. There I caught another flight to Brisbane, then on by taxi to the International airport where I boarded a 747 Air New Guinea plane for the final thousand miles of my flight. By the time I cleared customs it was late afternoon, too late to head for the office, so I went by taxi to the Islander Hotel. After coming out of wet and cold Melbourne it was like heaven. Many people may have considered it to be too hot, but for me it was just right.

The next morning at nine o'clock I met my new boss and his African born secretary, and outlined my strategy and objectives for training the local men in the safe use of gold mining equipment.

I wouldn't be flying up the jungle for a couple of days so I wandered around the locality, buying fruit and a small dictionary from the street market.

Whilst I was there I called in at the bank in Boroko and opened an account. It was a bank like no other I had ever seen. Standing menacingly in the doorway was a seven feet tall wooden naked warrior in full head dress plumage, with a massive spear and a penis most men would die for. As I was waiting for a teller to become free, hanging from the ceiling just above head height was a wooden crocodile about ten feet long with its back hollowed out in the form of a canoe, with six small children sitting upright inside. There and then I decided I was going to like Papua New Guinea. After three weeks I had become familiar with the section of road under construction between Tabubil and the Otmenga bridge. Some of the track was difficult and unstable even with a four-wheeled drive.

I found that some crane operators were neglecting their equipment but I soon rectified that with a warning. It did the trick. To improve on safety conditions I radioed Head Office with a request for wire rope lube packs to be sent to camp, and whilst I was on the radio my boss came on air. "Bob can you come down to Moresby, I want you to begin a Licensing program for gold mine operatives."

Thursday found me in Head Office, and later in the day I was asked to stay over and finish the job the next day. Friday came, and at about twelve o'clock the boss's secretary came over to me. "Bob you know that flight you should have taken this morning, well it's overdue, missing presumed down." The only person on that flight with the pilot would have been me! My guardian angel was, I believe, by my side that day.

The problem was that there was a large turnover of pilots, and the combination of low cloud, high mountains, and low flying non-pressurised aircraft, was a recipe for disaster. The jungle was so dense that the chance of spotting a crash site was almost impossible. I was a very lucky fella that day.

I had been told that if you, say, broke a leg and it was too cloudy for the choppers to fly, then you wouldn't get picked up until the cloud had lifted. If it was two days - too bad, they couldn't risk losing a chopper or the pilot. The guy who sometimes flew me around was a veteran of the South Korean conflict and I felt perfectly safe with him. He could fly me close up to any object with complete safety. When the cloud base was low he would follow the river along deep ravines, and it seemed strange to be looking down on large birds in flight, and huge stands of bamboo along the sides of the river up to forty feet high.

I was beginning to come to terms with the jungle and enjoy it - but it wouldn't last.

The project I was to be involved with, road construction, began after a two hour flight in a twin-engine fixed wing aircraft from Moresby to a small jungle settlement (Kiunga) and then half an hour on to Tabubil, a camp site which was perched on the side of a mountain. That part of the journey was taken by helicopter, usually along deep ravines, following the Ok Tedi river. The runway was too dangerous for fixed wings to land as a nine metre bank at the end of the runway didn't allow for overfly if there was bad weather or pilot mis-judgement.

We came in to land at Kiunga, and the pilot was guided in by someone standing on the airfield using a hand-held radio. There was always the danger of low cloud obscuring the pilot's view of the airfield, so it came as no surprise as we descended and came out of the cloud I could see what looked like long grass beneath the wing, but was in fact the tops of trees one hundred and eighty feet high.

We had just descended from two hundred feet of cloud, and after a couple of attempts we landed safely. During our descent there was silence except for the pilot and co-pilot talking to the man on the ground.

One evening I had tea in the cookhouse at the Otmenga bridge site. The cook was an old Aussie guy built like a brick shithouse, a real character. "Look at these Bob." He held out a fist full of twenty dollar bills. "In two weeks time I won't have a cent left" he began to laugh. "Ya know why - no - well I'm going on holiday to Manila, the same hotel I go to every year, and I'll have women waiting on me hand and foot, and everything else I want." With that he disappeared into the back of the cook house.

Time to move on. I started up the four wheeled Toyota, headed down to the OK Tedi river and doubled back along the causeway. Ten minutes later I was sliding and bouncing along the steep side of a mountain. Rain was pouring down and the light was beginning to fade. No!!

Suddenly I felt a jolt followed by a shudder, and I found myself facing uphill BUT going backwards as though I was in a slow motion horror film. A section of the road had given way and I was sliding silently towards the river. Trees and tall grasses were already floating on the river and stretching from bank to bank. I struggled through the door and onto the bonnet. I didn't want to be inside when it hit the water. 'How the fuck am I going to get out of this?'

I was sitting on the front screen looking back at the river as it got closer. 'What the fuck's going on, have I come here to be killed by a landslide, drowned, or eaten by crocs? - will they ever find my body, and what about my Cathie?'

The Toyota disappeared into the debris-covered river. I managed to get to the surface but my eyes were full of mud and I couldn't see a thing. Suddenly something struck me above my right eye, I reached out and grabbed it. Splashing water on my eyes I was able to make out the root of a large tree. It was taking me down stream like a giant battering ram.

"Don't splash about" I thought to myself remembering the crocodiles.

The light was fading fast. "What the devil am I going to do now?" The current was strong, there was no way I was going to make it to the bank safely. It seemed I was on the last journey of my life. Now I began to feel angry. "Got to get out of this mess - if I go to the right bank I'll be a goner, got to make it to the left bank to be in with a chance." Suddenly there it was - the causeway on my left, but the current was taking me too fast to make it. "Got to get to the left bank, what if I hit the bank, this tree will crush me, if I go too far past the causeway I won't make it."

There on the left bank, half in the water with its roots still embedded in the ground was a tree resting at a crazy angle and looking as though it might break away at any moment. "I must try to reach it."

I half swam half struggled towards it. The current took me under and my shirt was ripped off my back. As I was swept under the tree I managed to grab a branch and get my breath back. "No way am I going to die here, no way!" Painfully I hauled myself onto the upturned tree and just lay there, catching my breath.

The rain was still bucketing down. I was on the roadway where I dropped to my and knees and was violently sick. I didn't care, I was happy to be sick, it was a relief. I must have swallowed a fair drop of that muddy water. I knew where I was.

I could cut through the old dried up river bed which would be about two hundred yards and I would be at the cookhouse in ten minutes - but I'd seen crocodile tracks there a few days before so it was too dicey. Better to go an extra quarter of a mile and take the road that doubled back on itself up the hill. By now I was feeling really tired but somehow I kept going.

It was pitch black and the rain was still pouring down. I sat on the road outside the cookhouse, exhausted, like a wet rag doll. Mesmerised by the light glowing from the cookhouse, I felt as though all the energy had been drained out of me and I began to vomit violently. The hardest part was making it to the door. I yelled out "Cookie." For the next week I couldn't sleep for coughing, sweating and shortness of breath.

I felt really wretched and I was flown down to Moresby. The company doctor gave me a dirty look after I told him how I felt - I never looked ill even when I was. "Better get yourself up to the hospital, have an x-ray and bring the plate back here to me."

A short time later I returned and he put the plate up to an illuminated screen. Suddenly his whole attitude towards me changed. "Sit down Mr. Westworth, you have pneumonia, have you any other problems?" "Yes a couple of ulcers on my legs but that's about all." He broke a couple of phials and splashed the contents on my legs. "I'll make a report out immediately and send it to your Head Office." He needn't have bothered - I went back to Head Office and wrote out my resignation there and then.

Chapter 5
Return to Oz

Three days later I was back home with Cathie. The weather was warm and Cathie was wonderful. No more jungles for me. It's okay in those places if you're well, but illness can lead to complications. It took some time for my lungs to dry out but being back with Cathie was wonderful. We would have our quiet walks along the river, and in the space of four months I landed another job.

This time it was in Melbourne at the Footscray College of Technical and Further Education. I was employed in the capacity of Technical Officer seconded to the Braybrook Training Centre, Footscray.

There I instructed and licensed operators in the safe use of mobile cranes, forklifts and excavators. I remained with them for two years. I found the staff to be dedicated to their job, and I was happy during the time I was there.

I was instructing a group of NCOs on heavy lifting equipment at the Bandyanna army camp just north of the Victoria New South Wales border. The course ran from Monday to Thursday, leaving me Friday to return to Melbourne. On Wednesday of that week - 16th February 1983 - news reached us concerning the bush fires spreading from South Australia to Victoria, so in the evening I made a phone call to Cathie in Warburton. She told me she could see a red glow in the sky, it was over the township of Cockatoo, the rest of the sky was dark laden with ash from the bush fires, but she seemed calm. I'm okay" she said, and with that she ended the conversation and put down the phone. As she stepped out onto the balcony at the back of the house everything was eerily quiet. Suddenly the mountain opposite - Mount Little Joe - exploded into a sheet of flame, it travelled across the canopy faster than a galloping horse.

In a panic she packed the car with blankets, food and water, photo albums, dog bowls and our two dogs. Before she could reverse out of the car port an old Aussie neighbour stopped her, asking her where she was going. "Reefton" she replied. "Don't go, stay here, we've been in plenty of bush fires, if you need to move the police will tell you. Come and have a cup of tea." That old neighbour saved her life. Reefton was burned out that day. She would have driven straight into the flames.

We were lucky in that one of my young Aussie mates drove through the flames to protect her. He put tennis balls in the downpipes and filled the spouting with water in case any hot ashes blew onto the roof.

I had no idea of the drama that was unfolding - Cathie couldn't phone me because all the phone lines were down.

Early on Friday morning I headed to Melbourne and by late afternoon I was approaching Warburton. The road was blocked with Country Fire Authority workers and volunteers working hard to stop smouldering fires from re-igniting. They were smoke covered and so tired that they slept in shifts at the side of the road, whilst their mates carried on fighting the hot ashes and flames. There was a chow wagon serving sandwiches and drinks.

A police officer came over to me. "No-one is allowed past this point." He thought I was a sightseer. "I live in Warburton and I want to get home to my wife." With that he guided me past the water trucks and groups of men, and sent me on my way.

As I approached the river which separated our home on Donna Buang from Mount Little Joe I feared the worst. On the Warburton side of the river the beautiful eucalyptus trees had been reduced to smouldering black stumps.

I held my breath as I crossed the bridge to head up the side of the mountain to our house in Kent Street which was at the top nestled right against the forest, but it was untouched by the fires. Everywhere was green and fresh spoilt only by the ash-laden sky which gave everything a dark background.

As I entered the drive Cathie and our two bullterriers came to greet me. I hugged her and felt her beautiful warm body against mine. I loved her more than ever. There was no time for sleep that night!

In total the fires in South Australia and Victoria claimed seventy two lives. One thousand five hundred and fifty nine homes were burnt out. So much damage and so many lives ruined, millions of dollars worth of livestock killed. Pastures were burned out and there was no hay to feed the starving animals.

For months after the fires the birds that used to fly around the area were absent and everywhere was eerily silent. But soon the native trees had buds forming on their burnt stumps, and steadily life returned to normal.

During this time Cathie and I made lots of friends from all parts of Victoria, and I took pride in the fact that my instruction helped make people safe in the workplace.

It also had its rewards, such as the time I drove out to a fruit canning factory in Sheparton. The students, nine in all, were from the Maintenance Department.

The course lasted a week and as always it generated a lot of interest and was a great success. After loading all my lifting equipment onto the back of the college's low loader I headed back to Melbourne. As I drove over a rough back road I heard a rattling noise from behind my driver's seat, and fearing the worst I stopped, only to discover thirty tins of fruit. The men had put them there as a sign of their gratitude for my time spent with them.

At one of my classes in Braybrook Training Centre one of my students was a young Italian lad from the fishing port of Eden. He was very keen, asked lots of questions and showed great interest in the course. Needless to say he passed with flying colours. "Bob I want you and your wife to come and have a meal in my dad's restaurant, he'd like to meet you."

So on Friday evening Cathie and I set out, stopping en route at a pleasant motel. It was spotless and the evening meal was good. On Saturday morning we arrived in Eden and found the restaurant. The young man and his father were expecting us. "Sit down Bob, my father will serve a special fish dish just for you." It was a dish like no other, and we were treated like VIPs. "Here is a gift for you and your wife." It was a bag of freshly caught scallops, and to end a perfect lunch he added "You don't owe me a cent Bob, thank you for helping me with the course."

Later in the afternoon we said goodbye to the young man and headed home, once again staying at the same motel for the night. All in all it was a lovely weekend. What a wonderful job. I was happy and so was Cathie.

One location I travelled to was in Gypsland and some of my students were keen fishermen. The river had flooded and receded leaving large pools around two and three feet deep in low lying fields, mainly containing carp.

When the time came for me to return to Melbourne the men decided to take me on a fishing expedition, so very early in the morning I joined the party which consisted of three men and two dogs. As I waded towards a clump of tee tree bushes one of the men shouted "Keep out of there it's dangerous, snakes climb them to get out of the water."

After three hours we had a sack full of large carp. "Here are three for you Bob." I was grateful for them, and the experience was made all the more interesting by their fishing tackle which consisted of two dogs, one shotgun and two garden forks - not a single fishing rod in sight.

After two years with Technical and Further Education Melbourne it was their decision to relocate to Werribee to the west of the city. This would mean selling our home in the mountains and moving to a more populated area.

No more beautiful parrots, currawongs or lyre birds in our garden, or possums, wombats, deer or kangaroos with their Joeys near the house. It didn't bear thinking about so I sadly tendered my resignation, and the next twelve months found me working in the local area, but I just couldn't settle. I missed the travelling with all its challenges and meeting people.

There was a big difference between the city dweller and the down-to-earth old bushie in the outback. I always felt comfortable in their company. Cathie noticed that I had become withdrawn although I tried not to show it. At this time she had a job as a teacher's aide.

Life in the mountains was peaceful and relaxing, and often we would stroll naked in the garden. Most of the homes around us were holiday homes so there were no onlookers. We were free to do whatever we wanted - and we did. It was wonderful to be free and out of our clothes.

One day as I lifted a feature log from behind the carport, there lying underneath it was a snake about five feet long. Now I was very scared of snakes, so I shouted to Cathie "Snake!" "Kill it before it kills the dogs" she shouted. I couldn't. I froze to the spot as the snake slid silently under the wooden steps leading down into the garden. She was annoyed with me. "We have to kill it." With that she went into the house and produced a saucer of milk which she put near to where the snake had disappeared.

That was supposed to tempt the snake out but it didn't work. She started to rake the garden. I stood 'chicken' on the steps keeping an eye open for the snake, and after several minutes it re-appeared making its way slowly along the patio at the rear of the house. All it wanted to do was move on but the risk to our two dogs was too great and it had to be killed. I must admit I was useless in the situation. Sometimes snakes will hunt at night, and quite often we would walk bare-foot down the garden after dark. If we had accidentally trodden on one we would have been in real trouble.

"Cathie it's here" I yelled. She went down to the patio rake in hand, but due to the uneven surface, as she hit it all it did was to make it mad. It moved to attack her, striking at her with its mouth fully open missing her legs by inches, but Cathie was too quick and the snake lay dead. She put down the rake and began to cry. "Did you see its poor little face? I didn't want to kill it but I had to."

The next day she took it to school in a large jar for the headmaster to identify it. He said it was a Tiger snake, adding that if left untreated the venom kills within six hours!

Early in November 1984 I was once again searching the situations vacant columns of the Melbourne Age newspaper. One advert caught my eye.

'Wanted, Lecturer, aboriginal education, to instruct on heavy earthmoving equipment.' The job was to train aboriginal men on a road construction scheme six hundred and fifty kilometres south of Alice Springs. The Anangu Pitjanjatjara or AP offices were in Alice Springs. It was a one year contract involving the College of Technical and Further Education, Adelaide, South Australia, and was funded by the Community Employment Project (CEP.) I immediately posted off my CV not really expecting anything to develop, so you can imagine my surprise when two days later I received a phone call asking me to attend an interview at the offices in Alice Springs!

The flight tickets for Melbourne to Alice Springs via Adelaide and return, would be waiting for me at the Reg Anset flight desk in Tullamarine Airport. I was so excited - it was just the job I wanted. The next day Cathie dropped me off at the airport. We kissed goodbye and she wished me luck.

The first leg of my journey took only an hour. It seemed strange looking down at small dams on homesteads reflecting like miniature mirrors, and lots of greenery.

I could see parts of the main highway heading towards Adelaide, a route I had travelled many times - a journey that took eight hours by road. Here and there were puffs of white cloud hanging like cotton wool. Soon we were over the river Murray passing over the ferry at Tailum bend, then the newly constructed Murray bridge. We landed in Adelaide and after a short wait I boarded the flight to Alice Springs. This would take about two and a half hours. The same journey by road, as I would find out, took twenty hours.

We flew north and headed up the Spencer Gulf, passing over Port Pirrie and Port Augusta. There the scenery changed dramatically from the cool greens of Victoria to the white glare of Lake Torrens, then the Red Desert areas which seemed to go on forever. There wasn't a cloud in the sky.

Two hundred miles from Alice the pilot announced that if we wanted to send any messages ahead of our arrival we could do so as we were then within radio range. A short time later we were on the tarmac. The temperature was in the high 40s but I was comfortable with that.

I was driven to the AP office and began my interview. I sat facing a group of about ten elders and various office staff. They began asking me questions, but I felt uncomfortable. "Can you turn the air-conditioning off before we start, it's too cold for me." The elders laughed and nodded their heads in approval.

After the interview I headed back to Melbourne. I thought it had gone well, and I began to play over in my mind all that had happened. As I walked out of the Arrivals gate Cathie was waiting to drive me on the one hour trip back home to Warburton. All I had to do now was wait.

The days dragged by - then at the beginning of December I received a telegram. It was bad news, I had been unsuccessful. It was a body blow, I had been so looking forward to working and living with the aboriginal people.

The disappointment must have shown on my face. Cathie took the telegram from my hand and read it. She kissed me and whispered "You'll get that job." Strange - was it a woman's intuition or was she just trying to comfort me? To this day I don't know.

The days passed and I had resigned myself to the fact that I was never going to get the job, and then it happened!

On 21st December I received a telegram. "Please contact me on 089527078 regarding a position with Anangu Pitjanjatjara." Debra.

Chapter 6
Into Aboriginal Country

On 7th January 1985 I arrived in Alice Springs and called in at the AP office.

There I met the white road supervisor. He was in his mid fifties and had lots of experience in road building - that's what his CV said. He had towed his three berth caravan from Queensland accompanied by his wife. We were then waiting for the Mechanical Instructor to drive up from Tasmania, he would be there in another three days.

There were four office staff and Debra. At that early stage she was the secretary, but a short while later she would become the boss. She was smart, attractive and very knowledgeable in aboriginal affairs.

"I'll get you booked in at the Desert Rose Motel Rob and I'll see you tomorrow morning." With that I went and stowed my gear at the motel. Over the next twelve months I would make regular overnight stops there and become friendly with the owners.

The next morning at nine o'clock I called in at the office to clarify my strategy for the next twelve months and meet the rest of the staff. In the afternoon Debra had arranged for me to visit the flying doctor base for a first aid refresher course and get an overall view of how the system worked.

The rest of the week was taken up with collecting two new Toyota Utes (pick-ups) - one for the supervisor and one for me, fitting them with radios and long range water tanks. I also collected my swag (canvas folding sleeping bag, two blankets and a pillow) from elders IXL. After a week in Alice we headed south along the Stuart highway towards the aboriginal homeland where I would live and work for the next twelve months.

The first part of our journey to Erldunda and the Desert Oaks Hotel took two hours, then on to the hotel at Kulgera near the northern territory South Australian border which took one hour. After that the sealed road ended and the main highway became an unsealed dirt road. It took another three hours of dusty and pitted road to reach the aboriginal community in Indulkana. It consisted of one school, one garage, one store, a water storage tank, a small medical centre and about six single story homes not in use.

In summer groups of aboriginal people preferred to go walkabout from waterhole to waterhole. The older anagu lived in and near the town for medical reasons, i.e too frail to travel with the rest of the tribe on walkabout.

The Visitors Centre we stayed at had a kitchen but that was all. We slept on the floor in our swags and the next day we camped at Two Tanks. Around three hundred people attended the meeting.

Soon it was my turn to stand up and address the people and explain how I would train the men, assess them and help them to get their licenses for the vehicles we were using in the road program. It all went well and everyone was happy. That was when they gave me my aboriginal nickname Robbie Cowboy, because of my wide brimmed cowboy hat (a necessity in the desert sun.)

During the next couple of weeks the executive chose ten men to work on the road program. It was also agreed that if any of the men went walk about or had time off for ceremonial rites they weren't to be sacked. Remember this was aboriginal ground, anyone wishing to enter must have the approval of the executive and show a permit if asked to do so.

No cameras were allowed but I asked the executive if they would make a exception in my case and they agreed that Robbie Cowboy was okay as long as I asked permission off any of the men if I wished to photograph them. Otherwise I could wander anywhere as long as I didn't go on sacred ground (that was a definite no-no.)

The first man I was introduced to was Teddy, mixed race and in his early forties. Before shaking my hand he looked me up and down in somewhat of a cautious manner, then he let rip "You don't like the colour of my skin and when you white fellas came here you chained our men to trees, walked them in chains to Cooberpede, and sent our young women to Adelaide to learn white fella ways, our families were broken up."

With that statement he stood back one pace and studied my face as though expecting some sort of retaliation but it didn't happen.

I said "When I was a young boy the Germans dropped bombs on us back in the 1940s but I don't hold a grudge against the German people of today, it's not their fault, and as for the colour of your skin I couldn't care less if you were pink, blue, yellow or green, my job is to train you in the use of construction plant - and when my twelve months are finished I'll go home."

He stared hard at me, and then a big grin spread over his face. He stepped forward, put his arm around me and patted me on the back and began to laugh. "You'll do Robbie, you'll do." From that moment I liked Teddy, he was up front and said what he thought - much better than being two-faced or patronising.

There was Peter, in his late forties, chewed tobacco and stowed it inside his lower lip. Sometimes this habit caused cancer in tribal men. The younger men were David and his brother Jimmy. Tommy in his early fifties, a good hunter and provider for his numerous children. Snowy, a young buck who wouldn't stay with us very long. Sandy, always happy and laughing, in his early thirties. Another Teddy in his early fifties. Harry, thirty two years old, over six feet tall, great sense of humour - kept an eye on me and treated me as though I was his little brother. Colin the cook, ex boxer, early fifties, on the run from his little Latino wife who put the fear of god up him.

Leslie, a wonderful man in his early fifties - the man who adopted me, taught me the tribal ways and protected me, even putting his own life on the line later when I was attacked by a man wielding a Nula Nula (tribal fighting club.)

Often he would take me to his camp, and over a brew of black tea by the camp fire he would tell me stories. He would also take me walkabout, and teach me how to track and hunt animals. If I did something wrong or strayed onto sacred sites he would say to the elders "Don't be too hard on Robbie he's only an ignorant little white fella."

Finally - the road supervisor. He would cause trouble for me that would last until almost the end of the job. He was bad news.

During those first weeks we collected items of plant - sleeping caravans, ablutions van, mobile cookhouse, water truck, front-end loader, grader, tipper truck, two trailers, a low loader, Caterpillar D6 dozer, and a generator - all sent up from South Australia via the Ghan rail. The pickup point was called Chandler Sidings about three quarters of an hour south of Indulkana.

Whilst I was offloading the rail bogies the road supervisor insisted on taking the D6 on the low loader back to Indulkana. Due to the fact that I was quite busy I took him on trust to know what he was doing. "Okay but you must take someone with you and make sure the machine's chained on safely." "Yes I'll take Colin with me."

That evening I was about to settle down in the visitors quarters when Colin walked in looking hot and bothered. "Rob can you go to the low loader, it's bogged down in soft sand back near Chandler Sidings." "Okay no problem I'll take Harry with me." Twenty minutes later we drew up alongside the low loader. It wasn't bogged down as Colin had described, but the dozer was slewed across the deck ready to fall off. The only thing stopping it was a single chain. "Try and get the chain off Harry." As I slew it forward he quickly released the chain dog.

"Stand clear Harry and I'll try to slew it off over the side." Using full revs I managed to slew it squarely over the side, if I had just slid sideways the machine could have tipped over - we were lucky. We moved the low loader from off the sandy bank back onto level ground and re-loaded the dozer using six sets of chains. Had anyone been driving by and the chain had broken, they could have been killed.

As soon as I arrived at Indulkana I went to the so-called supervisor's caravan and blew the shit out of him. "Your job is to survey and align the road, not set a bad example to the men, my job is to train them in the correct and safe way on the equipment. You could've killed someone today." Obviously there were a few swear words thrown in. He didn't like it and in a couple of days he would get his own back in a sly and underhanded way (dirty sly bastard.) A few days later he began to show his true colours.

He called me to his caravan. "I've been told by the office in Alice Springs to give your Toyota to Tommy the co-ordinator, you will have to get lifts to go and see your operators, he needs the vehicle."

Tommy had also been told that he could use my Toyota to go hunting, and no-one saw much of him on site. It was a bad situation that would get worse with time. Reluctantly I handed him the keys, life was going to be difficult from now on, but if that's what the office wants then who am I to argue.

About mid February, before we started the major construction on the road between Indulkana and Mimili, Deb asked me to take ten of the men

48

to Marla Bore police station to obtain their provisional driving licences. This was in case they had to drive the tipper truck or low loader on the main highway - it wasn't necessary on the homeland as no licences were required.

The cop shop consisted of two containers converted into an office and lock up situated to the left of the Marla Bore Hotel motel which was a single storey. The left side was the bar and the building continued to the right with the reception and dining room. A veranda ran along the front of the low wooden building and behind that was a cook house and toilet block. A covered passageway went from the centre towards the back with a number of rooms on either side. There was also a shower in there. We could get a bar of soap and a towel from reception for a few dollars. It was about an hour's drive from camp.

I arrived about mid-morning with the men in two vehicles. We filled the reception area-come-office. It must have been an odd sight for the young cop on desk duty. Ten scruffy aborigines and a scruffy little white fella.

He called for reinforcements and an older cop came in from the office. "I've come to get these men their provisional licences." He viewed the scruffy bunch with curiosity. "Okay what are their names and addresses?" No-one answered.

The men began to speak quietly between themselves in aboriginal. He turned to me. "Do you speak their language?" "No." His curiosity was beginning to turn to bewilderment. The men were still talking amongst themselves. I knew they all spoke and understood English perfectly but I didn't let on. Very gradually the men gave their names with addresses as Indulkana. Everything was going well, that was until we came to Peter.

"Just a minute." The young cop went into the office and came out with a piece of paper and said to Peter "There's an outstanding arrest warrant out for you regarding a traffic violation. I'm afraid I'm going to have to arrest you." With that he put a pair of handcuffs on poor old Peter, who at that time looked worried to death. As he walked past me I asked the young cop "How long are you going to keep him?" He winked and whispered "He'll be out tomorrow." With that a grinning cop and a worried Peter disappeared into the lockup container.

When the men were sorted we headed back to camp. The first thing I did was to radio Deb to tell her that all the men had their provisionals. She went quiet when I told her that I went with ten men and returned with nine, but after a short while she saw the funny side. Some time later when the men were ready I took them for their tests which they all passed. I also went down there on a few occasions for a beer in my free time.

Most of the staff in the bar were young women, and conversation was easy. We would swap stories over a few drinks, and like the young jillaroos that worked at nearby homesteads they told me they were working their way up to Darwin.

One afternoon I walked out of the bar to order a meal in the dining room. As I approached the desk in reception there was a young aboriginal woman in front of me in a short dark skirt and a red top. Her skirt and top were covered in red sand as though she had been rolled along the unmade highway. Taking a bar of soap and a towel she made her way to the showers. "Could I order a meal?" I asked. "Yes, no problem, it may be a few minutes."

I made my way back to the bar and ordered another beer. Taking my time I headed back into the dining room and as I walked through the door a short fat little aboriginal woman squeezed past me - it was the one who had gone for a shower. She smelled lovely, and looking up at me she said "Hiya honey." I smiled and said "Hello." As she walked into the bar I couldn't help but notice that the arse of her skirt was still covered in sand, so was her top. I had to smile to myself.

Soon we had our first road camp set up exactly as the supervisor instructed, but due to the bad positioning of the diesel generator the men and I had sore throats and runny eyes. The diesel fumes twenty four hours a day were causing us to lose time at work. He was okay, his caravan was up wind of it.

Seeing what the problem was I went to him and asked if we could move the generator set from the centre of the camp. He thought it was funny and with a sneering grin, showing all his rotten teeth, his comment was "You can't help bad luck can you."

With that he went back into his caravan and shut the door. As I walked away I thought to myself 'this bloke's a real arsehole.' The next day he boasted to me that he was going to make the job go slowly in order to get another three years out of it and see him through to his retirement. I pointed out to him that he was on a twelve month contract to TAFE and after that he and I would no longer be here, but he wouldn't listen to me (what an idiot.)

It was decided by the men to work ten days and have four off. At ten o'clock the road crew would put on a brew of black tea boiled in a big old bean tin over a wood fire, usually on the side of the road. It was better than any cold drink. At dinner time I would get a lift back to camp with one of the men, but I was becoming concerned that I didn't have my Toyota with its radio, and if an emergency occurred we could be in real trouble.

At four o'clock we would all go back to the cookhouse for the evening meal. Sometimes after tea the men would light a camp fire and tell stories well into the evening, mostly in aboriginal, but if I was there they would speak in English. I loved every minute of it.

During the day I had accidentally brushed my right shoulder and back against what looked like a giant spider's web hanging low in a tree. Suddenly a nasty itchy rash appeared. It was driving me mad and I showed it to Harry. He poked it with his finger and frowned. "Tonight smoke." That was all he said. Later that evening all the men were engaged in conversation around the fire. He put a small bundle of twigs into the fire, and indicated me to stand up. Next he pointed to my shorts, then to the ground. "No." He pointed again and I looked at the men - they were deep in conversation.

I looked towards the supervisor's caravan, the curtains were closed and it was in complete darkness - okay he was in bed. I dropped my shorts and stood there completely naked. The men were still talking quietly amongst themselves and seemed oblivious to the fact that the skinny little white fella was standing there with no clothes on.

The next thing Harry did was to take the smouldering bunch of twigs from the fire and brushed them against the back of my head. I could smell my hair singeing. Then he brushed them across my shoulders. He lifted my arms and went down them, then across my back, across my buttocks and down my legs.

I thought that was it, but he made me turn round to face him.

He began under my chin with the smoke, it was choking me. I began to cough and my eyes were running like taps. I rubbed my eyes and for a brief second I could swear I saw Harry with a big grin on his face. Down the smouldering twigs went, to the tops of my legs. I was thinking to myself 'do be careful, don't burn any of my bits, Cathie won't be very happy if you do.'

At last he had finished. I quickly put my shorts back on and made my way over to the water storage tanks and washed my sore eyes. I didn't wash or change my clothes for two days and my bed stank of smoke. On the third day all my gear went into the washing machine and I had a good shower. Two days later the itching and rash had gone thanks to Harry and a few smouldering leaves.

Whilst I was working away in the homelands I didn't know that Cathie had caught viral pneumonia and was very ill. The doctors wanted her to go to hospital but she refused, telling them that there was no-one to look after our dogs. She stuck it out at home. She had already stuck it out through the forest fires of Ash Wednesday, and she would stick it out again. When she told me I was upset to think I hadn't been there to help her when she needed me.

The cause of the pneumonia was a mistake she made when feeding the parrots which would congregate in our back garden in Warburton. We had a clay short sided round shallow dish standing on a cut down tree stump. She said that one day she was in a hurry to get a couple of jobs done in the house, and when she put the seed into the parrots' dish she forgot to wash her hands afterwards. Obviously she would do this usually. By the time I came home on R and R she had recovered.

Her love of birds was undiminished by the experience. She even had a tame blackbird which used to sing on the handrail of the rear balcony, until one night a boo buk owl came along killed it.

When we went to bed it wasn't unusual to find one or two huntsmen spiders on the wall just behind the headboard. "Look Bob aren't they lovely, watch what happens when I turn the light off and back on." They had disappeared to goodness knows where.

Things Cathie hated were mosquitoes, although they never attacked her - march flies that made a loud humming noise and could give a sharp nip - and jumping jack spiders that lived up to their name. As we passed the lawn mower over their nests they would jump up and bite our legs. One day whilst I was away Cathie mowed the lawn and ended up being taken to hospital at Yarra Junction because of the jumping jacks. Not because of their bites, but because as she was trying to get away from them she almost cut the end of her finger off. She was trying to pull the mower off their nest while the blade was still rotating.

Oh yes, there was one more creature she was cautious of - it was the bull ant. We had been thinking of buying a building plot out in the bush and developing it, but as she leaned on a tree to get a better view of the sign she let out a yell. Her hand was red and swollen all day as a result of being bitten by a bull ant. Needless to say - we didn't buy the plot!

I didn't know that Leslie had adopted me until Teddy told me. "Why hasn't he told me himself?" He replied "That's the way it's done, it usually comes through someone, maybe second or third hand, but he will look after you, you are now his son." Sometimes uncle Leslie would take me away, teaching me aboriginal ways. One morning he picked me up at camp and took me walkabout for two days. It couldn't be for longer periods due to my work commitment. "Where are we going?" "One day at my camp just north of Sailors Well windmill, then to Mintabe to find some opal."

When we arrived at his camp he lit a fire and we had a brew. "Come on Robbie, I show you where eagles live."

He climbed up and sat in the nest. I was surprised at just how strong it was.

After that we went on more walkabout. We followed a narrow track to a small and almost dry waterhole.

"Can you see anything Robbie?" "Just a few tracks, what are they?" "Dingo" he replied. "Five in all, not been here long, can you see there's no loose sand on the feet marks - one was carrying something, see how the tracks are deeper than the others - they were in no hurry, see how close together the front and back legs are - maybe one hour ago." All that day he educated me as he would a young child, and I was grateful to him. "Look Robbie, the small hole in that bank, keep away from it, the track says a snake is in there, could be a king brown, maybe four or five feet long."

We moved on to a small tufted area where uncle got a small stick and began to prod the ground. Suddenly a centipede appeared, about nine inches long with a corrugated brown body, lots of legs and a black head in the shape of horseshoe.

"Be very careful Robbie don't touch it." "Why not" I asked. "It's very toxic, it won't kill you, but for three or four days you'd wish you could die."

That night I sat with uncle at his camp fire, and as the flames flickered and danced he began to tell me stories. "When I was a young fella" he said, "I worked as a stockman for iron bark Jim. One day I spotted a very young dingo pup. I jumped off my horse and caught him. I wrapped him in my jacket to keep him calm. I kept him for a short time - he was okay - then one day he left to live with the wild dingoes."

He went on with another story. "A group of aboriginal men went to a place where they sang men's songs in private with no women present. Whilst they were singing a young woman was nearby foraging for food and she overheard them. She went back to her camp where she met with a group of women who were also going out foraging.

Whilst they were out there the woman sang the men's song to them. One of the hunters came near to where the women were singing, and upon hearing the men's song being sung he gathered the rest of the hunters. They returned and killed all the women, or so they thought, but one young girl managed to escape by burying herself in the soft sand, and she left the tribe.

Approximately twenty five years later the now woman was relating the events in song and speech to the women in that tribe, when her husband overheard her. He gathered the rest of the men in the camp whereupon they killed all the women." I asked uncle if it was true, and as he stoked the fire he replied "Long time ago Robbie, long time ago."

I was so comfortable by the camp fire I could feel myself drifting off to sleep, but uncle had another story to tell me. I sat upright determined not to nod off.

This was the story:

'An aboriginal man was working at Kenmore Park and while he was walking he passed over a rabbit hole. Unbeknown to him in the hole was a wanambi, an invisible spirit snake, as big as a man. It whipped him with its tail, and one of its young jumped into his mouth. That night he fell ill.

In the morning he was getting worse so he was flown to the Congress hospital in Alice Springs.

He was there for three days, and when the doctors released him they gave him a small sack. "We have put the young wanambi in there for you. Keep him there and you'll be okay. Returning to Kenmore Park he put it on the back seat of his car. Word got around about it being on his back seat. He found he could leave his car unlocked anywhere, and no-one would break in or steal anything from it as they were so frightened of the wanambi.'

The next day he took me to Mintabe. The area had been divided up into claims and was being worked by bulldozers. At that time it was in its infancy. The flat topped hills were being reduced to white gleaming heaps of rubble. It was a sad sight and I could see the sadness in uncle's eyes.

"Come on Robbie, I'll show you something that will surprise you." He seemed to cheer up.

We drove for a short distance then he stopped and indicated to me to follow him on foot. After a couple of minutes he stopped. "What do think of that Robbie?" I stood there in amazement, I couldn't believe my eyes, he was right, it was a surprise. There in front of me was a small lake of fresh water about two hundred yards wide and five hundred yards long. It was about six feet deep in the centre. Scattered around its shore were a small number of humpies (aboriginal sleeping shelters built of branches forming a low tunnel, about four or five feet high and anything from six to twenty feet long) not in use at that time. At the eastern end was a windmill water pump which had long since stopped working - and there was one more surprise - a dozen well fed pelicans were bobbing up and down on the centre of the lake. I turned to uncle with only one question on my mind "How come this exists in this parched desert area?"

As usual he had an answer for me. "A long time ago a white squatter came here. We didn't understand why white fellas never helped each other, unlike the Anangu.

Our families help each other with food, water and walkabout from waterhole to waterhole, but the white fella never lived this way, so when their stock died they moved on." "But what about the lake?" I asked. "When the white fella left, the windmill stopped working but the cabi (water) still kept coming up through the ground."

I was back in Alice on 18th January and once again I had my digs at the Desert

Rose Motel room 27. During the evenings I enjoyed a dip in the town open air swimming pool. It was arranged for me to catch the Greyhound coach two days later back to Indulkana. That's when something very unusual happened.

As I was waiting for breakfast I heard a young woman with an accent which I instantly recognised as my own Midlands accent. She was standing in front of me as we queued for the coffee machine. "Excuse me where do you come from?" She turned to face me and exclaimed "I know you, tell me your name." "Bob Westworth." I had no idea who she was, but she seemed to know me. She threw her arms around me and began kissing me.

Everyone was staring at us and I could feel myself going red in the face. She hugged and squeezed me, "You're my dad's old mate. I'm Caron." Suddenly it became clear. The last time I had seen her was ten years previous - she was about nine years old. I remembered sitting her on my knee one evening and singing silly little songs to her after her dad and I had returned to his house from the pub. Then she introduced me to the three people who were standing next to her. "This is my boyfriend and his mom and dad."

We shook hands and they were as surprised as I was at our meeting. They were here on tour. "We went to Ayers Rock (Uluru) and the Olgas yesterday, and today we're going on a coach trip, and down to Cooberpede. Then on to Sydney and back to the UK." Our journeys overlapped by one hour and twelve thousand miles. This was the beginning of many surprises I would have there in Alice and the outback.

On one of my many trips to and from the homeland to Alice, uncle Leslie took me to a swimming hole turning west ninety kilometres south of Alice near a camel farm. I was learning something new every day.

"Come on Robbie I'll show you how we get fresh water for our brew." With that he began to scoop a hole in the sand about four feet from the water line. As the hole formed it began to fill with water, at first there was a fine scum on top, and after a short while it was filled with crystal clear water. We sat on the lake's edge watching the pelicans and enjoying a brew of black tea.

Once again we were moving on. Uncle was taking me to his own private spot where he occasionally dug for opal.

After ten minutes walking he stopped. "What can you see Robbie?" I was puzzled, the area seemed barren. "Nothing, just scrub and a dip in the ground." He laughed at me as he reached into the back of his four wheel drive. He pulled out a metal digging stick about three feet long and half an inch thick, hammered into a fan-like chisel. Poking it into a hole he came up with a lump of white rock and handed it to me.

On close inspection it had a beautiful seam of opal running through it. "You have it Robbie, and when you go home you can give it to your kunga" (wife.)

That evening we headed back to the road camp. All the men had gone on their four-day rest. I cooked our dinner, then went to bed in the comfort of my sleeping van. All in all it had been an interesting couple of days, once again being educated by uncle Leslie.

The supervisor had made it impossible for me to train the men in safety, always interfering and giving them jobs they weren't ready for. Also due to my lack of transport the men's safety was being compromised - I could no longer ignore the fact that he was holding the programme back. So with a heavy heart I wrote my resignation to Deb. On 21st February after packing all my gear I was having one last look around my sleeping van. The bed was tidy with clean sheets and blankets. They would come in handy for the next person. As I turned to go two of the road crew came in. I went to shake their hands but they pulled back.

This was most unusual as they were always happy - then one of the men spoke two words - yes just two words which would turn things around completely. "You stay." They stood there for maybe a couple of minutes then left. It seemed they knew what was going on, and my mind had been made up for me. I unpacked my bags and radioed Deb. She sounded relieved. "I want you to come up to Alice and see me."

The next day I was in her office. Once there I told her of the difficulty I was having with the supervisor and my worries concerning his interference with my training programme. She wasn't surprised at all, some of the men were unhappy with him and word had got back to her. "Try to carry on as best you can Rob and we'll see if we can do anything at this end, but it'll be difficult due to his position and his contract. I can't understand it, he has a very good reference from his last employer."

Alarm bells suddenly began to ring and I remembered what he said when he got Ted the mechanical instructor the sack - "Anyone can write their own references." "Okay Deb, I'll go back to camp and give it another go for the sake of the men." The next day he was quieter than usual, he couldn't understand why I'd returned. I left him guessing, and he seemed uncomfortable. I carried on training the men. They were happy to see me back.

On my day off uncle Leslie took me to his camp. He could see the tension between the supervisor and myself, and he gave me some advice. "Always talk to the snake's head, not his tail." In other words 'go above the supervisor's head.' I told him I had done so.

That night he told me more stories to take my mind off my problems. I sat there listening to him and felt as though I was in a different world, far away from my busy day to day routine. Sometimes, with a stick he would draw lizards, snakes and all manner of things in the sand near the fire. I would study them and learn their ways.

A story he told was of 'an aboriginal man driving to a township. He gave a woman a lift. She was wearing a long white dress. He felt uneasy and looked at her out of the corner of his eye. Then he could look at her no longer, he felt that she was a mumble (ghost or evil spirit.) He didn't take her into the settlement but dropped her off outside. He did his business quickly and drove off out of the settlement in another direction.

Just outside of another settlement approximately twenty miles away on a fork road he saw the woman waiting for him again. He drove past her too frightened to stop, convinced this time that she was a mumble. He never saw her again.'

All aboriginals have deep family ties. Fathers, brothers, brothers-in law, cousins etc. are all dependent upon the family unit. They lend or borrow things without any concrete responsibility to return it at any specific time, a fact that I would soon find out for myself.

Below our first road camp site there was a dried-up creek about twenty feet wide, and eighty yards from our camp. There were about eight camp fires down there. Tommy came over from the creek. "Robbie have you got any electric cable? I want to run it from the generator set to our video."

I took a look in our workshop trailer and came out with two rolls of cable with plugs attached. "Here Tom you can use these." I ran them down the creek to the television which was standing in the middle of the creek bed, and thought no more of it.

A week later I needed the cables for some work I was doing. "Can I have the cables back now Tommy?" He replied "No, you gave them to me." No matter how I tried, he wouldn't give me back the cables. He wasn't being awkward, in the tribal way I had given them to him, therefore they were now his property.

In the end I had to radio Deb to send me its replacement via the greyhound coach which passed through Indulkana on its run to Adelaide. I learned a valuable lesson that day and it was this - if anyone wants to borrow something make it clear that you will want it back.

I also learned about not playing my harmonica whilst on the homeland. One evening I sat on the steps of my sleeping van and began to knock out a few tunes. After a couple of minutes Tommy came running up - he looked worried. "Robbie don't play that." "Why, what's wrong?" "Playing music brings snakes." I put the harmonica away and didn't play it again. The problem was that if we got bitten by a venomous snake and had no access to a radio to call the flying doctor, we stood a good chance of dying in about six hours. One man was very lucky after being bitten. It happened a couple of years before I came on the scene.

Colin had worked his passage to Adelaide where he got as job as a barman. A group of unruly youths had been plaguing the place for some time before he took the job, and one day in desperation his boss asked him if he could do something about it.

Colin being an ex-boxer took up the challenge, but not in a way you would expect. Once again the mob came into the bar. What did he do? He called them over, told them the drinks were free and gave them each twenty dollars. Their tiny brains couldn't work out what was going on. After a couple of drinks he called them over to the bar. "Listen lads, you've had a few drinks and that cash, next time you come in you can pay me back." He didn't see them again. His boss was pleased, but he never told him how he did it.

He then moved up along the Stuart highway towards Alice Springs, working for a spread called Granite Downs. One day he was out checking stock with another guy. Now when you move through the low lying scrub you never know what is in there, especially if you're a white fella. Needless to say the inevitable happened. His mate was bitten on the ankle by a king brown Joe Blake snake - that's about as bad as it can get. No radio, no doctor, no anti-venom - but Colin saved the man's life. If the snake has disappeared that's that. If it's a female and you get in between her and her young, she will attack - but if you can't recognise the snake you must kill it for identification in order to select the correct anti-venom, but try to do it without getting bitten again.

The man had no options - the spot they were in was too remote. Colin lay him down on his back, took off his boots, took out the laces and tied them round his ankle - one above the bite and one below, this was a matter of life and death.

With an old razor blade which he kept in the brim of his hat he lacerated the bite area until the blood flowed, then he did the bravest thing of all - he sucked out the venom. If he'd had a cut in his lip the poison could have killed him. The man was crook (ill) for a few days, but he made a full recovery. Every time he saw Colin in Alice Springs he would call him over and buy him a beer, and another, and another until poor Col was legless, but he wouldn't say 'no' - he loved his grog too much.

He moved on into Alice where he shacked up with an aboriginal lady. That's when he saw the job advertised for a camp cook with the road programme. He had to move on from Granite Downs due to a little accident at a barbeque involving the owner's wife. He explained to me what happened. After a few beers he thought he would have a bit of fun. As she was bending over to get something to add to the barbie her big fat arse was too much of a temptation. He got a bull prod and prodded her. Now those things put out a very high voltage - if it'll move a bull on you can imagine the fright it gave her!

That's why Granite Downs and Colin parted company - but when he was sober he was the kind of man you would want around. He was dependable, and understood the aboriginal language. One day that would prove to be very useful.

Early on before we established our first road camp I borrowed some safety films from South Australia Highways Division. They were American orientated and were very good for getting the subject of safety over to the men - but one film in particular back-fired. It concerned a Caterpillar D6 bull dozer similar to ours being loaded onto a lowboy (low loader.)

The first point was the fact that the operator had forgotten to fasten his seat belt, and the second point was that the low loader wasn't on level ground, it was on a side slope and had a steel set of ramps and deck. The operator starts to drive the D6 up the ramps and as he gets onto the deck the machine slips over the side, rolls down a bank and kills the operator.

Now that may seem like a good safety point, but all it did was scare the shit out of the men watching it, and the result was that they would work the machine as I instructed, but when it came to loading up the machine to transport it, they insisted that Robbie put it on. It was months before they would load it themselves, but eventually they gained enough confidence to do it.

By the time my rest and recuperation in March came around I was looking forward to seeing Cathie.

I had been very busy, not only training the men but also keeping all our second hand machinery working. Due to the fact that we didn't now have Ted, the mechanical instructor, the onus was on me. Firstly the D6 dozer began leaking water around number two pre-combustion chamber. I contacted Deb, and she in turn contacted the Caterpillar dealers in Alice Springs. They were good enough to send me a new part with seals, and lend me the tool with which to remove and replace the old parts.

Shortly before I was due to get the coach for my R and R the Caterpillar 12e 17g grader had cylinder head problems. Deb was worried that the machine would stand idle until I came back. After a six hour trip to the Cat. dealers and an equally rushed trip back to Indulkana, I cleaned up the cylinder block, refitted the new cylinder head and got the grader running. I radioed Deb - she sounded relieved. "Thanks Rob, have a nice trip home and remember me to Cathie - I'll see you when you get back"

I finished the grader at twelve o'clock which gave me enough time to shower and get into some tidy clothes before catching the five minutes past six coach. I must have appeared somewhat of a curious sight with my tight dusty jeans and shirt, with my wide brimmed hat and leather boots with Cuban heels, carrying two hunting spears. One was made by uncle Leslie and the other by Tommy.

The coach bounced and ploughed its way south along the four hundred and fifty kilometres of corrugated and pitted unmade dusty highway which was still being used by heavy transport between Alice and Port Augusta.

It seemed strange that there was a road a short distance away running parallel to the one we were on. Parts of this road had been completed in eight months and parts were left unfinished due to government cost problems.

Suddenly the coach ground to a halt. The road was so rough that the gear lever selector had jammed and we were going nowhere. The heat outside was fifty one degrees and the air conditioning was off. I got out and found myself a shady tree. One hour later we were on our way. The 1695 kilometre trip from Alice Springs to Adelaide took twenty hours, and I was glad to sit for a couple of hours in the coach depot until it was time for the next 743 coach to Melbourne.

Eight hours later Cathie picked me up at the coach station, and an hour later we drove onto our drive in Warburton. I had been on the road for almost thirty hours.

During my first two days at home Cathie and I walked around the house and back garden naked, revelling in the privacy and freedom of our home on the mountain. We hugged and kissed like a couple of newly-weds. It was heaven after the dust and heat of the Simpson Desert. The birds were singing, the multi-coloured parrots were noisily squawking in the tall trees, and the honey eaters were collecting nectar hovering around the trees and shrubs. In the evening possums and wombats passed near to the house.

After a few days we found time to service our two cars and catch up with some painting and maintenance around the house. We also caught up with some old friends in mount Evelyn. They were a large Italian family and often invited Cathie and me to their family gatherings.

During this time I contracted a nasty bout of flu. There was no way I could return to the homeland because the aboriginal children had no immunity to it. Their noses would run like taps and in some cases it could be fatal. Eventually my doctor gave me the all clear, and at nine thirty on the evening of 17th March I boarded the coach to Alice via Adelaide. Whilst there I called in at the TAFE college to catch up on their involvement with the road programme.

I arrived at Indulkana on 19th and almost before I stepped from the coach someone put his arms round me and gave me a great big hug, almost knocking the wind out of me. The man with the big smile on his face was uncle Leslie. "Palya Robbie" he shouted. Taking a quick look back at the coach I saw all the passengers staring wide-eyed at my reception. It was good to be back. He drove me to the road camp and the men were happy to see me again. I felt at home in their company.

All the men had to be off the road by three o'clock on 22nd due to watis (men) in cars going to the next town on men's business (coming of age rituals.) Usually they blocked off the road to everyone at that time. If anyone was on the road during this period (usually three days) there could be a death in that person's family, or one of the relations could suffer the same fate.

We had been making a road into the scrub for a water drilling rig to enter next to Kangaroo Dreaming Ground. I had no transport and had to rely on lifts from the men.

After sorting out who drove what, the supervisor announced that he was going to operate the D6 dozer and level the pad for the drilling rig. I wasn't happy with this idea. The machines were for the men to use. This was what the programme was developed for. I told him so but he completely ignored me.

When I arrived at the site the pad was three feet out of level causing the rig to jack itself up, making it difficult for the men to work. By then I was getting really pissed off with this arsehole. The next time I spoke to Deb over the radio to order a fuel delivery for the camp and a few spares for the machines, I told her what was going on with the supervisor.

She was annoyed with his meddling in the men's training - not only was he putting their safety at risk he was putting the whole road programme in jeopardy by holding back its progress, and there was a danger of it being cancelled. Now it was Deb's turn to get pissed off. It came to my mind again about him once saying "Anyone can write their own references." "Deb can you give me the name and phone number of his last employer?" She pulled it out of her file and gave me the information. "Ok thanks, over and out."

The next day uncle Leslie drove me to the phone at Chandler Sidings. After a while I got through to the company and gave the person the name and reference of the supervisor. There was a short silence.

They wouldn't have a bar of him and went ape shit. "The creep was here for two months and we had to sack him." It was music to my ears. I phoned Deb and told her what was said. Her only comment was "He's got to go."

I was sitting under a tree by the cookhouse one evening when I saw a movement in its lower branches - it was a black snake. By now thanks to uncle Leslie's teaching I was able to live alongside these creatures and accept the fact that they were a daily occurrence.

When I went to bed that evening I put my mosquito net over my bed, because when we had the occasional rain the insect eggs in cattle droppings and wild animal droppings came alive, carrying germs including meningitis.

I went for a walk a few days later with the last film in my wide angle lens camera. I found quite a few rabbit burrows and one on the side of a thirty foot slope about an hour's walk south of the camp. All I had with me was my camera on a strap, and I was wearing a brief pair of jocks. Suddenly I wasn't alone - a large shadow caught the corner of my eye. I turned and faced the hillside where the shadow was slowly and silently gliding. I was staring straight into the face of a large eagle.

He was gliding on the air current about eight feet away at head height, moving from side to side. I reached and took the lens cover off my camera - as I did so I noticed his mate coming in from my right in an almost vertical dive. I was in trouble. The only thing I could do was to face each one as it came in at me. I was swinging my camera by its strap over my head. The two birds swerved sideways and up. They glided about twenty feet away and came in once more.

The best form of defence is attack, so I ran at the one heading for me, shouting and swinging my camera - it banked smoothly and gracefully missing me by about three feet. I was thrilled by its beauty, its piercing brown eyes that never left mine. During the time it came at me and as it moved away, I was thinking in split-seconds. A few graceful strokes of its wings and it spiralled up to my left to about thirty of forty feet. The menacing part was the eerie silence of these large birds - just their steady movements, their bodies silhouetted against the blue sky, their large talons, the menacing curved vicious beaks and the hypnotic glare of those piercing eyes.

Quickly I looked to my left. The bigger of the two birds was gliding towards me again about ten feet high and fifteen feet away, and closing in rapidly. I was working on sheer reflex and instinct then. I dropped onto one knee and held my camera up to my eye. There was no time to focus, he was about ten feet away and closing in. I had him head on in the lens, but his mate was still circling about thirty or forty feet up. Click. He was still closing in, his head was moving from side to side and he seemed to be suspended in time.

The sinuous under-side of his wings stood out like a painting, the wide and soft tail, the large talons and that magnificent head with its fearsome flesh-tearing beak. For a second I was mesmerised. Once again the camera was going round and round on the end of its strap - I still had my lens cover in my left hand which I was waving in the air. About five feet from me he broke into an upward movement, I felt the air-flow from the powerful wings. Instinctively I slipped the lens cap back on and started to walk back down the hill. All the time I was wanting to run but dared not. The smaller of the two birds went back to the crag on the top of the hill above the rabbit holes - 'so far so good.' The larger of the two glided from side to side about thirty feet above my head, then by making a circle he dropped down about twenty feet and came up in a direct line behind me.

This time I resorted to hurling stones at the large shape, but I couldn't hit a barn door at five paces! All the time I was walking away, turning to face him at the same time. Then I noticed his mate had come back to join him, so once again I was faced with the two of them.

'How far are these two going to follow me before they lose interest?' By then I was about a hundred and fifty yards from the initial onslaught site and heading back towards the road camp.

I spotted a piece of stick about three feet long, it seemed like ages before I reached it. Picking it up I held it above my head and turned quickly to face them. I was running at the big one shouting like a mad man - it did the trick. The smaller one broke for the south and the big one was then at least keeping a respectable distance from me. I hit the stick on the ground as an act of aggression, but to my horror it disintegrated into dust. Then I threw a stone at him. He watched it as it went over his head and down to the ground, then his gaze returned to me. After about another sixty yards he banked gracefully to his right and returned to the crag.

I was still looking over my shoulder as I entered camp. What had I learned that day? Next time carry a gun if only to make a noise! - and get more film! Uncle Leslie said that I was a very lucky young fella. Wedge-tailed eagles kill young kangaroos by grabbing their shoulders with their talons and ripping their throats out. The wing span of the large bird was about nine feet, and the smaller bird about seven feet.

Our opening ceremony to celebrate the beginning of the road scheme took place in a dried up creek bed a few hundred yards north of Indulkana. There were a number of aboriginal elders there, and at mid-day about a hundred people (anangu) turned up. It was all very informal. The Minister for Aboriginal Affairs attended and made the usual political speeches, after which a very enjoyable event took place. 'The kangaroo hunter's dance.' They called it a dance - but it was an old tribal story re-enacted for the benefit of the Minister and the children. There were four men playing the hunters, and one man the kangaroo.

Before they started the men had to take up their positions on the dried-up river bed. Uncle Leslie turned to me, "Robbie look away until the men get into position for their dance. Although you are my son you are an uninitiated man." I did as he said and after about a minute they were ready to start. "Okay Robbie you can look now."

It was great fun, with the crowd shouting to the hunters and pointing to the man taking the part of the kangaroo - but he was cunning and every time the hunters got near him he would escape, causing roars of laughter and lots of clapping from the audience. After about fifteen minutes the hunters caught the kangaroo and went through the motion of dispatching him with their hunting spears. Then everyone clapped and the men in the audience began to stand up and sing songs.

As the time went on, people who were sitting in the shade of some gum trees moved around, keeping within the shade area. I noticed on the side of one of the trees there was a bare patch on the trunk, about four feet long and three feet wide where bark had been removed.

"What's happened there?" I asked uncle. "Someone's taken it to make a baby carrier out of it, they can also make bowls for carrying berries and other fruit." Again uncle was educating me. At about four o'clock he drove me back to camp. Everyone was happy, talking about the meeting and the dance songs. It was a good dance by the anangu.

The next day a bad dust storm lasted all morning. I had to put an up-turned empty bean tin on the exhaust stack of the D6 to stop the manifold being filled with sand. We all stayed in the cookhouse, it was the only place that was dust-proof. When the storm was over I went into my sleeping van and found that the bed had a layer of sand on it, so did the clothes in my locker. I had to shake my blankets outside and sweep out the van. It had been impossible for anyone to move during the storm without being blinded by the force of it, it was so bad.

A few evenings later I unwittingly exposed my bare body in the shower block to a large dose of Mortien fly repellent.

I was trying to get rid of the blowflies - not realising that I was allergic to the chemical. I felt ill all night and in the morning it was much worse. Trying to take my mind off it I decided to cut the legs off my light blue overalls which I'd been planning to do for some time, but things were going from bad to worse.

There was a terrible pain in my chest, my breathing was getting difficult, I had a red sore rash all over my body and my palms and the bottoms of my feet were itching so much that I was scratching them until they were red raw.

It was ten o'clock and the camp was deserted due to days off. The only transport I had was the tipper truck. In a desperate attempt to find medical help I drove it out of the camp towards Indulkana. After a short distance I couldn't even change gear I was in such pain. The truck came to a standstill, I could go no further.

Chapter 7

My life saved by a Witch Doctor

Sometime later, with ever increasing sickness, I spotted a dust cloud in the distance - it appeared to be a car coming my way. In desperation I fell out of the truck and landed heavily on the dusty track. I attempted to walk towards the car but my knees gave way. It stopped and a man stood over me. "Are you okay, what's wrong with you?" he asked. I looked up and saw that it was a police officer. I was lucky. It was a patrol on one of its rare visits to the homeland.

I heard them say something about the flying doctor but I needed medical help much sooner. "We can turn round and take you to the medical centre at Indulkana, but that's all we can do." I was lifted into the back seat of their Toyota personnel carrier, and after a bumpy ride I found myself on the wooden steps of the medical centre.

The officer pressed the bell, got into the Toyota and drove off, leaving me doubled up on the platform. After what seemed like ages a young woman in her early twenties came walking from the rear of the building. She took one look at me and said "Tell me what's wrong and I'll go and relay it to the nurse. She's in bed with a crook back." 'That's great' I thought to myself 'that's all I need.' Anyway I told her my symptoms, plus the fact that I was violently sick and couldn't even keep a glass of water down, and I had a headache that was so bad it was beginning to affect my vision.

The nurse's bungalow was at the rear of the building. A couple of minutes later the young woman returned. "The nurse has diagnosed an allergy rash and you must have Mylanta anti acid, hydroform cream and a sleeping pill. She opened the front door to the centre and steered me into the first room on the left, Ward one, with a large observation window looking out into the corridor. "Rub this cream all over your body where you can, and your private parts. I'll send a male helper to rub it into your back." With that she disappeared.

A young aboriginal guy came in and straight away he recognised me. "Robbie are you okay?" (what a question!) "No." "What's wrong?" That's when my wicked sense of humour kicked in "Maybe a wanambe." His eyes opened wide "Do you want the witch doctor?"

At that point I would have welcomed anyone or anything to get me out of my suffering. "Owa" I replied. Uncle Leslie had taught me that 'owa' means yes, 'jingaroo' means maybe, 'palya' means ok.

Ten minutes later a small thin man arrived. It was Alji the Indulkana witchdoctor wearing a blue and red beanie, blue denim jacket which had seen better days, blue jeans, sneakers, sporting a short grey beard and heavy brown-rimmed glasses. He walked sedately into the ward. By this time there was a small group of anangu in the room, and about eight or nine children with their noses glued to the observation window. The helper told him my trouble. He came over to my bed and began to massage my stomach in circular movements and, in complete silence, drawing my skin into his cupped hands as though pulling out some invisible influence.

This went on for maybe a couple of minutes, then he closed his fists and dropped his arms to his side, turned and walked to the door. One of the men opened it and he disappeared into the dusty street and out of sight.

After a short while the witch doctor returned and repeated the process. He did this four times and to my surprise the pain was getting less intense. He returned for a fifth time and the young helper said "Show him exactly where the pain is." I pointed to the spot on my stomach.

He stood at the end of my bed and began to chant for about half a minute, then touched his forehead with the closed fist of his right hand. Once again he came to the side of my bed and I pointed to the spot where the diminishing pain was. He held his hand palm down about six inches above my stomach, and something very strange happened.

I had the feeling that electricity was coming from his hand and passing into my stomach. After moving his hand from side to side he seemed satisfied. Taking one step back he spat on both hands, rubbing them together vigorously, then stepped forward and began massaging my stomach for about two minutes in the spot that I had indicated. Then he did his usual thing, turned around and walked away (that was it.)

Before he came into the room I had been sick, could neither stand nor sit without a lot of pain, my breathing had been laboured and my vision was becoming blurred.

Now the nurse's assistant gave me a big mug of hot tea which I drank with no problem. "Do you want a dinner?" she asked. My thoughts went to the old people who used the centre for meals. "No thank you" I replied. "The witch doctor is good" she said. "He fixed my neck when I was crook, but he won't do the head, you have to go to Alice Springs for that."

The next day when the men returned to camp I told them of my experience with him. They all agreed that he was good and only did good things.

Sandy was very pleased, telling me that the witch doctor was his uncle. "But you must be careful because there are also fierce witch doctors who do bad things." A fact which I would find out for myself before my work there was finished.

He also told me a story about 'the gudarchi man (feather foot) a killer who was paid to murder people who'd done something wrong. He stalked at night naked and no-one could hear him creeping up on them, although he wouldn't hurt children.' Anangu used to make small camp fires at night with two sticks pointing together so that the gudarchi man (mamu or mumble as he was sometimes called) couldn't see them from a distance. Also he travelled in willi wills (small whirl winds) and was invisible during the day. Once a fact, but then just a story from the past. He was active up until eighteen years before.

This story was told by the road camp fire at about seven o'clock in the evening. It was getting dark and there was a cold chill in the air. The very mention of the gudarchi man was enough to make all the men sleep with their lights on - they were shit scared.

One afternoon as I was returning to camp after checking out the men's progress, I drew near to a small group of aboriginal women who were sitting in a circle deep in conversation. I waved to them and they waved back, so I stopped to talk to them. I was learning so much about these wonderful people through casual conversation and today would be no exception - but the lesson would be totally unexpected. As I neared them they gave me a smile, but I didn't sit amongst them. I had been accepted by the Pitjanjatjaraku - the people of the Pitjanjara. They tolerated me in much the same way as they would a curious child, so they were comfortable to let this little white fella stand and listen to them. They knew they had my respect.

They weren't speaking in aboriginal or English, in fact they weren't speaking at all, but never-the-less they were deep in conversation.

Back in camp I forgot all about it, but a couple of days later in the evening uncle Leslie took me to his camp and the conversation turned to the small group of women I had met earlier. He said that when a woman's husband dies she will not speak, everything she says is in sign language. This will last for a long time - maybe a year, that's our custom"

I noticed that some of the men sometimes used sign language, as did Harry when he wanted to stop me. He made a fist and banged it down as though on an imaginary table. I understood what he meant and stopped immediately.

They must have developed this sign language over thousands of years and I was a really lucky little white fella to have been treated to this very clever means of communication.

The night sky seemed to be filled with shooting stars, and the Southern Cross was clear to see. I felt as though I was lying under a giant star spangled blanket. The camp fire was warm and comforting and I was always happy to be with uncle in camp. I knew it wouldn't be long before I was fast asleep. He poked the fire with a stick bringing it to life and making shadows dance on nearby rocks.

"Robbie, I'll tell you a story about the Southern Cross and the leader of a tribe called the Kanda tribe. He was a very old man with four daughters. One day he called them together. "When I die my spirit will go into the night sky, and I want you girls to come and meet me there." He didn't want to leave the girls unprotected against forced marriages to men who they would not be happy with, and this would be arranged by a wise witchdoctor who lived many days walk from their camp in a certain direction to which he pointed."

A short time after telling his daughters this the old man died, and the sisters began their journey to find the witchdoctor. After many days of hard and dusty travel they found the old witchdoctor, knowing their fathers request he took them to his camp, in a corner was an enormous coil of grey rope which he had made from his own grey beard. He pointed to the sky and the rope began to rise up until the top disappeared into the night sky. He told them that if they wanted to see their father they would have to climb up the rope.

They were frightened to climb so high but he told them it was the only way they were going to see him. So carefully they began to climb - higher and higher.

When they reached the top they found him waiting for them. They became four stars we call the Southern Cross, and close to them is a bright star - that is their father looking on at his four girls.' Uncle went quiet and as usual was waiting for my reaction.

"What do you think Robbie?" I looked up into the night sky and gazed for a long time at the Southern Cross. "I think that's a wonderful story uncle and I realise how important dream time is to the aboriginal people." I felt that he had educated me once again and I loved every minute spent with him in his camp.

He told me that when he was young his uncle took him hunting. He was going to teach him how to hunt malu (kangaroo.) After tracking for a long time they came across a big old red 'roo standing on a low hill in front of them, just about in rifle range. He was so big he had a head like a horse. His uncle indicated for them to get closer and when he was satisfied they were close enough he motioned to Leslie to aim for the centre of its chest.

Carefully he aimed and squeezed the trigger. It seemed to have no impact as the old kangaroo just stood there. Leslie whispered to his uncle "Do I shoot him again?" "No wait." After a couple of minutes the kangaroo fell sideways dead. "Always aim for the chest, never a head shot - that's classed as a dirty shot and could lead to a death in the family." (payback.)

The eldest male or father of the family always eat the brains of the kangaroo as it will help him to grow more wise and clever - like the kangaroo.

Another good food is a goanna (large lizard two or three metres long.) He is the best bush tucker. The emu is also a good tucker, but Teddy would never shoot one, he believed the emu was the spirit of his dead relatives come back to check on him and make sure he was okay.

Uncle had called in as I was sitting on the steps of my sleeping van feeling fed up. I was getting nowhere with that awkward stupid supervisor. He came over to me and said "Come on Robbie, you look tired, I can get a good fire going in my camp and we can sit and talk." It was peaceful without the noise of the camp generator, and it was comfortably warm by his camp fire - so much so that I drifted off to sleep. I wasn't disturbed by him, but after about an hour I woke up and was feeling a lot more at ease. He boiled some water in the billycan and we had a brew.

"What's wrong Robbie" he asked. Unbeknown to me he had been watching me as I slept and in fact had been watching me all day. I told him the problems I was having with the so-called supervisor. It was obvious that he and all the men knew what was going on between us. "I think the men will listen to you but not the supervisor - we don't want him here. I'll talk to the executive, maybe he'll go away."

Something must have been said because Deb called me on the radio and told me in no uncertain terms that Tommy must not be allowed to use the Toyota at all, and he must hand the keys over to me. It was clear that something was going on at the office - the men had been ignoring the supervisor and he was beginning to feel uncomfortable. He began going to the doctor at Indulkana on the pretence of being ill through stress, and during this time he told the men that he was going to cut their time if they were late. This was against the agreement between TAFE and the Executive, and Teddy told him if he did that he could stick the job up his arse.

He'd caused trouble for me by handing my Toyota to Tommy. I had to ask him to give me the keys back and he became hostile towards me, but I couldn't blame Tommy for his reaction.

He gave instant notice to quit shortly after this but I asked him not to go. He was a good man and I wanted him to stay, so I told him to go sick two days before the break and come back after he'd had time to calm down. It was my job to hold the men together if the programme was to be a success. He got his sick note the next day. At the same time a new mechanical instructor, Billy, came on the scene from Queensland - smart young fella in his late 20s, good mechanic, but not very experienced in man management. This would soon lead to his downfall.

When driving on dirt road in the outback you could be hundreds of miles from medical help, so even a minor accident could be fatal. Therefore there are a couple of golden rules I always followed.

One - Never drive flat out round blind bends.

This happened to me one day when young Billy was driving my Toyota. The tracks were humped and covered in loose gravel and we had gone round a couple of blind bends too fast for my liking.

I reached over and took the keys from the ignition making us slow to a stop. Billy was livid. "What the fuck did you do that for?" "You're going too fast round the bends." "But there's no traffic on these homeland roads." "How do you know?" I asked. He went quiet. "There may or may not be traffic on the road but you can't be sure.

I'll tell you something else Bill, if we were to hit a kangaroo or a bullock the Toyota could roll, maybe resulting in broken bones, or worse still a cut artery. It takes six hours to drive to Alice. Another thing, IF we could get hold of the flying doctor he could be anywhere in the territory and could be hours away."

He didn't comment - he just sat there. I handed him the keys and we carried on our way at a much more sensible pace. I taught him a lesson that day.

Two - Never drive off until the dust has settled after a vehicle has gone by.

A lot of outback roads can be as straight as a die and you can see for miles, but that doesn't mean you're safe or can relax. If you see a dust trail in the distance and it's heading your way, it may seem to take ages to reach you but before it does you must pull over carefully to the side of the road. I say carefully because there could be deep pot holes covered in dust deep enough to break an axle. You then let the vehicle drive past. It could be a car or a truck with three trailers behind it - it takes about a mile for the trailers to stop. Never drive off until the way is clear for you to see.

People have been known to pull out as soon as the trucks have gone by and they've been killed by a following vehicle which they couldn't see. That rule applies day or night.

Colin and Billy took the Toyota to Granite Downs to pick up some meat supplies for the freezer to keep the men going until the end of the ten day working period, also some animal rib bones for the anangu camped nearby.

At four o'clock I switched off the generator for it to cool down so that I could carry out a maintenance check. Tommy came up at four thirty and asked if I would start it again because he had his video playing in the dried up creek. I did as he asked. Later he asked me if he could borrow my Toyota for picking up the kids to take them to camp from Indulkana. "Okay" I said "but be back for six o'clock."

I didn't want to refuse him, it would seem childish. He did return at six o'clock and he was happy - and so was I.

Next day uncle Leslie borrowed the Toyota to watch a football match - there was no way I could refuse my uncle. Tommy came in at tea time and had a packet of tea, and Teddy came in for some diesel for his car.

We had a bad rain storm - it had started during the previous afternoon. The rain fell with such force that it blew through the vents in my van and forced the door open - my bedclothes and bed were soaked. The only dry place to sleep was the cookhouse so I moved in with my canvas swag, but first I had to step over Harry who was snoring his head off near the counter. He had the same idea as I did but got there first, but there was plenty of room. I lit the barbeque grill to dry out some of my gear.

Before that I had radioed Deb for a few spares for the vehicles in camp - also to give her a list of men who were ready for their truck tests. There were still one or two pieces of kit outstanding which were coming up from Port Augusta via the Ghan railway.

"The supervisor came back to camp late last night" Colin said, "and when I checked the freezer this morning two loaves of bread were missing and the meat had been moved about - the bones weren't in the centre of the freezer and it looked like something had been taken out. Tommy says the executive are going to give the supervisor the flick."

I told Tommy that I thought Teddy would make a good supervisor, and asked if they would put him in the job. He told me that was the plan (brilliant.)

We went around the back of Indulkana by the water storage tanks, at the rear of a slight bluff. There was an old caravan standing there with a good chassis. As soon as I could I would take our Hough front end loader and burning kit, and take the body off the chassis to make a water trailer for Tommy.

On the way back to camp on the narrow sandy road, we saw a blue and white Volkswagen coming towards us. As it went past Tommy said "I'm not allowed to talk to that man." I asked him what he would do if his car broke down. "He would have to get his kunga to tell me, then go into the bush away from the car while I fix it." Tommy and the man couldn't travel together or be in the same room - this situation was decided at birth, that's the tribal way.

The tribal way when anangus die, uncle Leslie had told me, is that they are seated at the entrance of their humpy, and friends come and sit face to face with them. They tell them what's going on in their lives, then say goodbye. Each person in turn does the same. Normally they view the deceased for one day, but depending on where people come from, it could take three days for them all to visit.

They find a good spot and dig a round hole about five or six feet deep, depending on the ground conditions. They arrange the body in the foetal position and lie it on its side, then fill up the grave and put big trees or rocks on top of it. They would visit the grave on a daily basis for three days, to make sure no goannas or dingoes had dug up the body. On the third day they would scatter the logs or rocks covering the spot, mound up the soil or sand, and, duty complete, they would leave.

Deb radioed me to visit the office on 11th May. I stayed the night in the Desert Oaks Hotel at Earldunda on the turn off for Ayers Rock, where I was introduced to the owner and his wife and their two young children, a boy of seven and a five year old girl. Whilst their mom and dad were busy running the hotel they would wander out into the nearby bush in search of horned devils (small spiky lizards) and bring them back to the hotel to keep as pets. It wasn't without its dangers however, as the young lad explained. On one such expedition he was bending down peering into some low scrub and as he parted the grass he came face to face with an angry hissing death adder. He was so scared that he ran flat out back to the hotel. He was a very lucky lad because death adders have enough venom to kill a horse with one bite, and without quick treatment a person would die.

After breakfast I set out on the last part of my journey, and two hours later I arrived in Alice Springs. The town was busy with tourists making it difficult to find a room for the night. Luckily the owner of the Desert Rose Motel whom I knew well was able to fix me up with a last-minute cancellation. Next morning at ten thirty I was strolling down the high street when who should I bump into but uncle Leslie. His eyes lit up when he saw me and he gave me a big hug. "Come on Robbie." "Where are we going?" I asked. "To the races, we can walk there, it's down by the gap (a broken rock formation at the south end of the town.) When we arrived there the place was full of tourists.

"Robbie we can see the start of one of the races." Uncle grabbed my hand and pulled me along. As I looked at the starting line I was amazed to see all the runners squat on the ground whilst their jockeys mounted them. It was a camel race! He saw the puzzled look on my face and began to laugh. "Didn't you know they would be camels?" "No I had no idea."

After spending most of the day together we went our separate ways - uncle to the Old Timers, I to the Desert Rose. Following a nice evening meal I went for a walk around the town then back to my digs for a relaxing shower and bed. The end of a perfect day.

The next day I collected Colin and we went to the super store for perishables, cabbage, bread, butter, cheese etc. to last the men for the next ten working days.

We then headed south and after two hours we stopped at the Desert Oaks Hotel for a couple of beers - the Toyota had no air conditioning. He introduced me to the head cook. A man of about forty years old, stocky, round faced, dark curly hair and hands like shovels - and he was as mad as a wheel.

Next we made for Kulgera and after an hour we were in the bar of the hotel downing a few jars. Then it was time to begin the three hour journey on the rough unmade corrugated highway back to Indulkana and the road camp. There I was greeted by young Bill. "The supervisor says he's stopping your camp allowance Robbie." I wasn't too bothered, he would soon be on his way out.

That evening I went with uncle Leslie to his camp and once again he was educating me in the ways of the anangu. We had the usual tea by the camp fire then the conversation turned to hunting spears and he told me how they were made.

Some hand spears are made out of young mulgar - mainly short fighting spears. Throwing spears are made from special trees, the anangu whittle down the shaft to suit their hands and push them into the hot sand around the fire.

When they are hot they take them out of the fire and roll them on their knees to straighten them. They make the point out of mulgar wood - they make it flat, split the end of the shaft, then get a dried kangaroo back leg tendon, chew it and bind the end - when it dries it gets tighter.

Uncle seemed to know when I was feeling a bit low and always found something to talk about. It was as though he had a sixth sense. Despite the fact that we were born into different cultures and in different parts of the world he seemed to read me like a book. The man had all my love and respect. This is one of the stories he told me as we sat by his camp fire.

'One day early in 1982 during the rainy season a bloke was fishing off the footbridge by the Riverside Hotel in Alice. He had a fish nearly two feet long on his line which had come out of his deep freezer. He would sit and wait till a group of tourists came by and start to heave on the line as though the fish was putting up a great fight. He would do it for five or ten minutes then pull it out of the water. When the tourists had gone he would throw it back in and wait for the next mob to arrive. The sale of fishing rods in Alice was good that day, all the tourists bought a rod and reel. Unfortunately the river was down the next day so nobody got to use them'

We hadn't seen Harry for nine days since he collected his pay cheque. He kept getting pulled back to Alice and wouldn't be back until he ran out of cash. One afternoon I was in the Stuart Arms having a beer with him at which time he had five hundred dollars in his pocket. Then along came one of his three wives and put the word on him for a new gear box for her car. Then came another one and put the word on him for something else.

By the time evening came he was broke. I bought his beer for him and gave him twenty dollars to tide him over until he got back to camp. He was a real character - always laughing and he never let anything worry him.

The supervisor was still making things as difficult as possible for me. He arranged for Colin to take the Toyota to Alice on his next four days break, but it backfired on the sly bastard. On his return journey to the homeland Colin picked up four aboriginal men and by the time he stopped at Kulgera everyone was well oiled. One of the men driving the Toyota stole some rabbits from the rabbit catchers ute parked nearby. At that time there were only two dwellings at Kulgera, one was the pub and opposite was the cop shop.

As the men were about to leave a large hand reached into the Toyota and removed the ignition keys. "Okay which one of yuz has taken the rabbits out of that ute?" There was silence. Once again the big old cop spoke "I know one of yuz has taken them and if I don't see someone put them back yuz all going to be locked up. Slowly and silently one of the men made his way to the ute and put the rabbits back. The cop seemed satisfied with this and put the keys back into the ignition, but pulled back quickly. "Yuz can't drive, yuz smell like a bloody brewery."

He looked at Colin sitting in the passenger seat "Yuz look like the only one capable of driving, have yuz got a licence?" "No" he replied. "Doesn't matter, can yuz drive?" "Yes" said Colin. "Then get into the driver's seat and go, if yuz come back here I'll lock the lot of yuz up." Somehow Colin got back to camp and the perishables looked as though they had been trodden on by a herd of stampeding horses.

The old cop must have traced the registration number back to AP Roads because the next day Deb called me. She wasn't pleased. "Robbie you know you work ten days and then have four days off? Well from now on you'll spend the first two days in camp and the next two days you'll pick up the cook and collect the provisions for the camp. I don't want a repeat of what has just happened." "Okay Deb that'll be done." I wanted to ask her a few questions but thought better of it. "Anything else Deb?" "Yes Robbie I'll arrange digs for you for the nights you spend in Alice. Over and out."

Teddy said it would be cold when the seven sisters come up in the sky from the east - so when I spoke to Deb via the radio, besides the fuel order and the men's wages I put in a request for extra blankets.

At tea time uncle Leslie once again took my mind off my problems in camp by telling me the hunting techniques used by the aboriginal women when out hunting for food. As always he had my full attention. He began "Women gather fruits and certain roots of plants and they catch rabbits." He produced a metal rod about half an inch thick and three feet long, with one end hammered flat to form a fan shaped chisel. "This is a digging stick they use to prod on top of the rabbit hole. When they dig through they get a dry twig, spit on the end and push it into the hole and twist it. If rabbit fur is there they dig towards it, if not they keep prodding the ground until they find one. Educating me again.

I went up to Alice with Colin by coach. Twenty dollars and ninety cents each way. We left Indulkana at ten thirty in the morning and arrived in Alice at four thirty. Deb booked me in at Toddy's Cabin for one night, cost twenty four dollars. The next night was spent at the Desert Rose.

The supervisor was causing real trouble by doing just what he wanted regardless of Deb's orders. By then I was really pissed off with the arsehole, therefore before I left I wrote a letter of complaint and gave it to Deb.

On my return trip with Colin he seemed to be ill and getting worse by the minute. He was drinking a lot of Coca-Cola from a large bottle, and he was sweating and having trouble communicating. When I got him off the coach at Indulkana he was having great difficulty walking, and fearing he could be having a stroke I took him up the steps into the medical centre. I caught the eye of a big butch nurse. "What's wrong with this man?" I told her his symptoms, and fearing the worst I asked if he could stay there overnight for observation. She looked into Col's eyes, smelt his breath and went ape shit. "He's not staying here the night, you can bloody well take him away, he's drunk."

I couldn't understand what was going on, all he was drinking was coke, then I smelled the bottle! It turned out that he had poured the coke away and filled it with Bacardi rum. Somehow I got him back to camp via a lift off one of the men, steered him into his sleeping van and onto his bed. He lay there looking like he was dead. The next morning he didn't surface, so guess who cooked breakfast for the men. Yes - me! That was the first time I cooked a meal for them but it wouldn't be the last.

The two water tanks mounted on one of the trailers were leaking after we had moved on to the next camp site - due to the fact that they were tall tanks and the swaying of the water loosened the bottom seams. We did a temporary repair but it was becoming obvious that they weren't designed for mobile use. The availability of water was also a problem, we had to arrange with Mimili when it would be convenient for us to take water from the settlement water storage tank. They had to pump it full the day before we collected it. If, as sometimes happened, the water pump broke down, it could well be a two-day wait.

The water in the Simpson desert, the Aborigine homeland, varied in quality. Some looked clear but was unfit to drink, some was brackish but okay, some had too much calcium and the result was a type of mould appearing on our teeth. Throughout the time we were on the road, water or the lack of it, proved to be a major problem. The water tanker was designed to spray water onto the surface of the dry road we were building to help with compaction, but it was decided to take the sprayer bar off the rear and fit a water supply pipe to the ablutions van and the cookhouse, and scrap the two unsuitable tanks.

Joy upon joy! The supervisor and his wife left today 29th May. I read the telex of his resignation and gave copies to Teddy and the men. They were very happy, it was as though a big cloud had been lifted from us.

Whilst waiting for a replacement supervisor Teddy would be doing the job, this was decided the previous day by the executive. I contacted Deb and confirmed that he knew about his promotion. She added that the supervisor had tried to wheedle out of giving in his notice, so the company solicitor had to do some quick talking to get rid of him. This meant extra work for me - training Ted regarding men's wages and the general running of the camp and decisions concerning the road construction. However I knew that he could handle it and it would result in him becoming a permanent supervisor. I was as happy as the men were that we had at last got rid of a nasty sly underhanded individual.

Things were soon returning to normal. Bill was teaching the men on the principles of the diesel engine, and I was still instructing and assessing the men on their operating capabilities, and organising their driving tests with the help of Deb in the AP office. Teddy was still working the D6 dozer, and in between I was guiding him through his new role as supervisor.

After ten days of work I was looking forward to spending two peaceful days watching camp, one day travelling up to Alice, and the next day returning with Colin and the perishables. So after checking over the generator set and topping it up with fuel I would start out on my trip to Alice at three o'clock in the morning in order to arrive at nine o'clock - drop off my overnight bag at the Desert Rose, and head off exploring the country around Alice.

Sometimes in life things happen that are totally unexpected, out of character and beyond our control. That day was going to be one of those times.

I had found a water hole about half an hour's drive west of the town on the Hermonsberg Road and a short distance off the highway. It was about two hundred yards long and sixty yards wide, and in the shape of a half moon. A large rocky outcrop at the back gave it some shade and there was a two-seater wooden bench near the water's edge.

After living on the tribal homeland it wasn't unusual for me to swim naked in the occasional water hole and even walk about in the nikiti (nude) at and around camp when it was deserted on rest days. It was a fact that the occasional tourist would visit the spot, but after having a good look around I came to the conclusion that no tourists were within the area.

Off came the stubby shorts and I waded into the water, it was warm until I got into deeper water then it went cold due to the shade from the rocky outcrop.

After about ten minutes I felt that I'd had enough and decided to swim back to dry land, but before I had a chance two young women appeared. The shorter of the two was carrying a guitar and sat on the bench. She began playing her guitar and they started to sing in harmony, they sounded like real professionals,

It was obvious neither of them had spotted me. After a couple of minutes I began to feel cold. "Excuse me, excuse me." They stopped singing and turned their attention to a head bobbing up in the centre of the pool. It must have come as quite a surprise to them. "Excuse me, could you let me have my shorts, they're on the bench, you've been sitting on them."

The taller of the two stood up and held them out to me. "There's only one problem, I don't have any swimming trunks on." I half expected them to walk away but they didn't, instead they laughed. "Don't worry we'll look the other way." Hesitantly I made my way towards them - I was glad to be out of the cold water. Plucking my shorts from the woman's hand I stepped into them and had scarcely got them above my knees when they both turned around to face me.

I dragged them over my wet groin as quickly as I could - they could see I was embarrassed and began to laugh. I sat on the bench and they explained that they were American university students on vacation, and staying at the Desert Rose Motel.

The woman with the guitar sat down next to me and began to play country and western, while the other stood in front of me singing and swaying to the music. It was wonderful, and as she moved the breeze pressed her flimsy white dress to her body exposing every outline, leaving nothing to the imagination. She was breathtakingly beautiful. I felt myself getting excited and looking down I covered my embarrassment. It was too late, she had already seen it and to my amazement all she did was to smile and carry on singing. After a short while they decided to take a walk around the pool and when they had gone a few yards I turned awkwardly and waved them 'goodbye.'

I got into the truck with great difficulty. The trouble with stubby shorts is that they're no protection or cover in this sort of situation. It was crippling me trying to get into the driver's seat so I took them off and drove naked until it had gone down. After a while I was able to get out of the truck and put them back on. Lesson learned - don't swim naked in pools where tourists may turn up!

Another embarrassing 'stubbies' incident was when I was travelling back to Indulkana one day, following a visit to Deb. I was reading some mail which I had received from TAFE Adelaide. The journey was much more comfortable than driving the Toyota, and I could spread my legs - heaven. Once again my attire was in the order of sandals, a light short sleeved shirt and my stubby shorts.

After a while I sensed that someone was watching me - at the time there were only about a dozen passengers on the coach. On the other side of the aisle sat a very attractive woman in about her mid forties - short cropped black hair, light blue top, dark shorts and a pair of legs that seemed to go all the way up to her neck. She smiled at me and appeared to be intrigued that such a rough-arsed bushie could read, and her curiosity got the better of her. She moved across the aisle and slid onto my seat pushing herself up against me.

She introduced herself and said that she was an exchange teacher from America living and working in Adelaide. I told her I was living with the aborigines and explained my work with them. She asked me if I was Irish!

All the while we were chatting her legs were tight up against mine and they were hot. Almost two months had gone by since I felt a woman's legs against mine and they belonged to my Cathie. I felt myself beginning to sweat. I looked down and to my horror something was beginning to appear as if by some sort of magic from the right leg of my shorts - it was clear it had a mind of its own. I held the pages of my letters over it hoping she hadn't noticed, and thinking to myself 'I hope this goes down before I have to walk off the coach.

I drew my legs up but all that did was to make matters worse, it was as if part of me was being strangled. She carried on talking, giving me her phone number and telling me I would always be welcome to visit her. I found out that day that American women can be very tactile - it was something I wasn't used to. By the time we reached Indulkana everything had settled down and I was able to walk off the coach with my shirt and shorts intact - what a relief.

One of the men told me about one time when his wife went out on a shopping spree. When she returned she saw a man's legs sticking out from under the car. His willie was sticking out of his shorts and thinking it was her husband she tucked it in and gave it a little pat, then carried on into the house.

A few minutes later a red faced mechanic with a bump on his head knocked on the door and handed her his bill. His wasn't the only red face that day.

At ten o'clock on the morning after my encounter with the girls I went to pick up Colin at an address on the outskirts of Alice. After knocking on the door for some time I decided to go in as it was unlocked.

There must have been a hell of a party the previous night because there were pissed bodies strewn all around the floor - Col was in the middle of them flat out on his back and snoring his head off. I managed to pick my way through to him and get him into a sitting position. "Come on Col time to go shopping."

Slowly his eyes began to open and it was plain to see that he hadn't got a clue what day it was or where he was. "Come on Col it's Robbie." He began to look around the room at the bodies and his eyes slowly came into focus. I helped him to his feet but he didn't move straight away. Very gradually I steered him over the bodies still deep in sleep, out of the front door and into the passenger seat of my Toyota. He was steadily gaining consciousness and by the time we got to the super store he was able to utter the occasional sentence. He grabbed a customer trolley and used it as a walking frame wobbling from side to side between the rows of produce.

Luckily I knew by heart the items we needed and so about fifteen minutes later we headed for the checkout. By this time Colin's eyes were beginning to glaze over and he was hanging on to the trolley for dear life. "Is he

okay?" the woman on the checkout asked, "only he looks real crook."
"Yes" I replied "I think he's had a heavy night."

As the produce moved along the belt I steered him into position and began loading up the trolley. We had an account there so the only problem was getting to the Toyota. As the cashier handed me the bill there was an almighty crash. Colin had passed out and fallen flat on his back still desperately holding on to the trolley, catapulting all our provisions back into the store. Everything stopped.

The workers on the checkouts stood on the counters to see what was going on, and all the customers gazed in bewilderment not knowing what was happening. I tried to pick him up but he was a dead weight and had a death grip on the trolley handle. Fortunately a man came over and helped me get him somewhat unsteadily to his feet. I held him upright while the cashier and a couple of customers refilled the trolley, then steered him to the Toyota. After wedging him into the passenger seat I off-loaded the trolley and drove out of the car park with customers and shop staff roaring with laughter. The next job was to collect dry ice from an industrial unit to shovel into the bags with the chilled items.

Two hours later I stopped at Desert Oaks for a refresher and by this time Col was beginning to look almost human.

He wobbled into the bar muttering something about 'the hair of the dog.' After half an hour we left, and an hour later we stopped at the hotel in Kulgera. He downed a few more beers, then we left for Indulkana and the road camp. Three hours later we arrived in camp and Col staggered to his sleeping van. He managed to get up the three steps and collapsed on the bed, completely wrecked. Guess who did the cooking for the men the next day - yes it was me again!

Deb was due to visit us and I picked her up at Marla Bore. I took her to camp and on site where we were cutting a new road parallel to the old one and she was happy with our progress. I made up a bed for her in one of the sleeping vans and Colin cooked her a nice meal. All the men were happy to see her. She was a good boss and we intended to look after her as though she was one of our own.

I also took her to the previous camp site to give her an idea of the distance between set ups. We would complete five kilometres of road, move the camp five kilometres beyond our finished road, then continue the road construction five kilometres beyond our site - thus working in ten kilometres stretches.

Uncle Leslie gave her a handful of opal that he'd dug from his secret place. She was surprised at just how the men respected her. The men also gave her boomerangs and shields which they'd made especially for her.

The next day was taken up with Deb, travelling down to the quarry and observing the men as they worked. Stone was being loaded to build up low spots by a crossing at Amaroona Creek. She ate with us at breakfast, lunch and teatime. Colin couldn't do enough for her - the meals were brilliant.

Soon it was time for me to take her back to the hotel at Marla Bore where she was to catch the coach to Alice the next morning. She had her overnight bag with her, and I had brought shorts and a clean shirt. After the dusty trip we were both ready for a shower and change of clothes before eating.

We found her room and I prepared to take my shower - the shower room was down the hall. "Deb do you mind if I change in your room after I've had my shower?" "No problem Robbie." I had a shower and put on my clean gear.

By now we knew each other well, like an old married couple only without the sex. I sat on the edge of her bed waiting while she showered and changed.

We went into the dining room and relaxed over our meal and a few glasses of wine. By then it was getting late and I had to get back to camp. "Come on Deb I'll see you back to your room."

I was worried about some rough men from another road crew playing up in the hotel. Once she was there I was satisfied, and almost an hour later I was back in camp.

In my early days on the job I realised that there would be a lot of overtime required of me concerning maintenance and mobility of the second-hand equipment we were using. It was agreed between TAFE and myself that no monies would be paid for the hours and days I worked in overtime. They would be accrued and taken in extra days for my rest and recuperation, also that any extra time at the end of my contract would be taken off my final leaving date.

I was happy with this arrangement - it meant that the total days for my rest and recuperation in June/July would be fourteen.

I told Teddy that I would be taking my R and R on 20th June. He gave me a big grin and put his arm around my shoulder. "Robbie you've been a good help to us, don't travel in your own time travel in ours." He took me completely by surprise. With those words there was no doubt in my mind that he and the men appreciated my efforts, and he was in my opinion going to make a fair and honest supervisor.

Taking Teddy's advice I phoned Cathie for her to organise a ticket from Indulkana to Melbourne via Adelaide, leaving on 18th June. Late in the evening of 20th she came and picked me up at the Greyhound coach station. She had brought our young black bull terrier Sally with her - the other one Billy was left at home. Sally had a tongue like a file and insisted on giving my face a good wash.

An hour later we pulled onto our drive. It was good to be home with my beautiful wife - my lover and my friend.

My first job, when I eventually got around to it, was to drive into the forest and cut enough wood to last through the winter months. Whilst I was away Cathie had a new free-standing log burner installed in the lounge. It was like a piece of heaven after the damp and cold of the outside.

One afternoon we drove to the top of Mount Donna Buang and as we approached the top the early snow was falling, making driving difficult. Soon coming into view was the fire fighters' observation tower and the undercover barbeque centre. No-one was there - it was so peaceful and quiet, a far cry from the heat and dust of the Simpson desert.

We stayed there for maybe an hour walking through the falling snow. The dogs were having the time of their lives charging through the snow that was already about a foot deep - in and out of the tree ferns drooping with the weight of the snow. It was great to see them happy.

After an hour and drinking our flask of tea laced with a taste of whiskey dry, we decided to drive slowly and carefully down to the valley floor - a journey of around fifteen minutes. Whilst on the snow covered road we saw lyre birds darting across in the half light. It was a magical sight with their upright tails and their dark bodies silhouetted against the white background. As we reached the valley floor and approached Warburton the snow gave way to cold miserable rain. We crossed the river Yarra bridge and doubled back up the lower slopes of Mount Donna Buang to our home just below the snowline, and into a nice warm house. The dogs were happy just to stretch out in front of the log burner. Cathie and I cuddled up on our large comfortable settee - we weren't going anywhere. We went to sleep in each other's arms. A perfect end to a perfect day.

Whilst I was at home there were lots of jobs around the house for me to complete, and lots of new and old friends to be visited.

I was still a certified examiner for the Department of Labor and Industry, and when the men working on the Lillydale to Yarra Glen Railway Restoration Project got wind that I was home, I found myself at the Yarra Glen station carrying out a test of one of the men in order for him to obtain his backhoe front end loader licence. It went well and I wrote the appropriate paperwork to be processed at 500 Burke Street, Melbourne.

Whilst I was there I had a couple of beers with the guy in charge of the station. He told me it should be completed in about two weeks time, ready for the first train. They had done well considering that they had to repair long sections of wooden trestle bridges across the Yarra river with nothing more than hand-operated cranes mounted on rail bogies, and hand tools.

To show his appreciation he gave me a car load of red gum logs cut out of old railway sleepers. They give good heat and burn very slowly similar to our oak - ideal for Cathie.

Time seemed to fly by and once again she drove me to the coach station in Melbourne. We hugged and kissed - it was time to say 'goodbye' again. We missed each other but she accepted the fact that this was how I earned my living.

The return journey would take three days because I had to stop over in Adelaide and call in at the TAFE college to discuss how the AP road programme was progressing. I heard a rumour there about trouble in the road camp concerning young Billy and Tommy. I didn't have a clue just what it was about but I knew it must be serious because there was to be a big meeting within the next couple of days at the camp. The Executive and TAFE representatives were to be there, and I was asked to attend. I sensed that there was going to be big trouble.

Meanwhile, next day, on a return trip from Alice to the homeland I was accompanied by uncle Leslie. He didn't drink alcohol so it was a dry run. He was like a camel, he could go without water over long periods.

We were travelling at ninety kilometres per hour over the rough corrugation of the unmade highway - corrugation occurs on sandy untarmacked roads. It's like the ripples on a beach as the tide goes out. If the road isn't graded smooth at regular intervals these ridges occur, much like a ploughed field - mainly at right angles to the direction of travel and up to four or five inches deep, rather like the corrugated plastic sheets on a shed roof only bigger.

One hour south of Kulgera at this speed the vehicle was stable, any faster or slower and we would have drifted off the highway into the ditches on one side of the road or the other. As we approached a bend uncle pointed and said "Stop there Robbie." "Why this spot?" Everything looked the same, dusty banks on either side of the highway, low scrub and a few trees scattered here and there.

He got out and walked about forty yards up a low rise to the east of the highway and stopped. As I drew level with him I was amazed at what I saw. It was a small lonely little grave pointing north-south, well kept despite all the dust and sand surrounding it. At its head was a cross with the details of the person buried there, and arched over the grave was a slim tree covering the length of the grave as though protecting the young child's last resting place.

Even more surprising was a glass vase there filled with water and fresh flowers. I was puzzled. This was a remote area with no visible landmarks

91

that could be seen from a passing car. "How come the fresh flowers?" I asked uncle. Pointing to the highway he told me that some of the truckers passing by knew of the grave and would stop to put water and flowers on it.

As we got back into the Toyota uncle said he had another surprise for me, but it was about another half an hour's drive south. Once again we were bumping and bouncing along the unmade Stuart Highway and sure enough, after half an hour he pointed. "Stop there Robbie." As we came to a standstill I looked around at what was just another featureless part of the dry desert - or so I thought. Again we were on the eastern side of the highway. "Come on Robbie but be careful where you walk. After about five minutes he came to a standstill, and I could see why he had told me to be careful.

In front of us the ground was dotted with holes that had been dug by hand by prospectors some time ago. On average they went down about fifteen to twenty feet and were just wide enough for a man to get down into. Near one of the holes was a rusty windlass with a thin round metal hand crank, and the rusty remains of a galvanised bucket standing where it was last used and abandoned.

Uncle studied my face to see my reaction. I was bursting with curiosity. "What were they digging for?" He bent down and picked up something green and covered in dust from one of the mounds near a hole, and handed it to me. "Jade Robbie." "Why aren't they digging it now?" He pointed to the piece I was holding. "Low quality." Then he added "I know where there's a mountain full of top quality jade." "Where?" "About one hundred and twenty kilometres west of Alice." "So why don't they dig it out?" "Because it's in a sacred place and we don't talk about it." He pointed to the jade I was holding in my hand. "You take that and give it to your kunga next time you go to Melbourne."

After taking one last look at the diggings we again headed south for the last hour and a half of our journey back to camp. I was lucky to have him pass this knowledge on to me - he was so nyindi (clever) and I remember it to this day.

The meeting regarding the trouble with Billy and Tommy took place on Friday 19th July. There were eight members of the Executive present with their leader, a representative from TAFE Adelaide, a homeland advisor, all of the road gang, Deb, Colin and myself. It was spoken mainly in

Aboriginal and as the meeting progressed Colin translated for me. Tommy told them that Billy, in a fit of temper, took the tyres off one of the Toyotas, including the spare, and burned them in order to stop him using the vehicle. The tyres were valued at three hundred dollars. As the meeting came towards the end Colin began to look worried. He turned to me and in a whisper said "They're going to call you to hear what you think. Whatever you do, don't let Billy come back, I fear for his safety."

Sure enough they called me into the centre of the meeting. "Robbie for you we speak in English. Billy burned tyres and upset everyone, what do you think?"

What could I say? I had no idea what had gone on in my absence, and as far as I knew young Billy had always appeared to be a pretty decent sort of guy. Really it was between him and Tommy. Remembering what Col had said I glanced towards him - he looked more worried than ever. Everyone was waiting for an answer. His words echoed in my brain 'whatever you do don't let Billy come back, I fear for his safety.' I turned to face the Executive and the words came tumbling out of my mouth as though someone else was saying them. "I think Billy should go." This was Billy's downfall - lack of man management.

It was the end of the ten day working period and the camp was deserted. As I passed the radio shack I heard my call sign - it was Deb. "Can you come up to Alice tomorrow, there's something I want to discuss with you. I've got you booked in at the Desert Rose for three days - over." "Okay Deb, see you about mid day - over and out."

Throughout my six hours drive my curiosity was building. It was just after lunch time when I walked into her office. She made me a coffee with milk - just what I needed, she must have read my mind. The drinking water in Alice was so saline it caused tummy problems - different from the homeland drinking water.

She sat down beside me. "After you get back from the cook's run I want you and Ted to come back here with your overnight bags, because we'll be going to Adelaide on the afternoon flight for a meeting with the State and Federal Government and TAFE regarding the grant for next year. I need your advice in order to present them with a list of plant requirements and running costs." That was where my three years as a demo operator and installation engineer came in useful.

"Okay Deb, it's like this - ask for a little and you'll get half of a little. Ask for a lot and you might get half of a lot." She laughed. "Okay what do you suggest?" "Two twin-powered motor scrapers, two water tankers, better access to water by drilling more wells, and two self-propelled multi tiered rollers - plus fuel. You could be looking at well over a million dollars." She began to smile. "Do we really need all that?" "No, but it'll give them something to think about."

Five days later Ted and I walked into her office sticky with sweat and covered in dust She handed me the keys to her house and said "Both of you go and have a shower and tidy up, I'll see you back here in an hour and we'll catch our flight." We made the most of her shower, her perfumed soap, and a drop of scent. Chances were we must have smelled like a couple of brothel owners.

When we got back to the office I handed Deb her keys and she laughed. "You're not so much on the nose now."

We went by taxi to the airport. As we headed across to the waiting aircraft Ted suddenly stopped in his tracks. "I've never flown before." "Come on Ted, I've flown stacks of times, it's okay, you'll be sitting by me." It was time for me to put my arm on his shoulder for a change. "Come on Ted." We got into our seats - he was sitting across the aisle from me. "You okay Ted?" "Yes" he muttered in a half choked voice. The plane taxied for a short distance then we took off.

I could see the colour draining from his face and his knuckles were turning white as he grasped the armrest - and as the aircraft lifted into a steep climb, instead of relaxing in his seat he was stooped forward rigid with fear. Two hours later we landed in Adelaide. His colour had returned and he was much more himself. "Good on ya Ted."

We made our way to the meeting which was held in a private room within the college. In all there were seven or eight people sitting either side of two joined-up tables. It began with the usual introductions. Ted and I were questioned about the progress being made, and estimated targets for the next twelve month period.

Ted was on the ball - I sat back and allowed him to answer for himself, after all he was the new supervisor. Deb also gave them the estimated plant and running costs, including wages. They went very quiet. Had I given her the wrong advice?

Before we got up from the table the Director General of the college complimented me on my choice and training of Ted. I felt so proud that my hard work had paid off - what a compliment, and in front of everyone!

Deb and Ted carried on with a private meeting. She told me that she'd been given a grant of five hundred thousand dollars for the next year. "I can manage with that" she said with a grin from ear to ear like the cat that got the cream.

After twelve thirty my time was my own, so I decided to explore Adelaide and sample a few beers. One beer led to another and one pub led to another, until the inevitable happened. I placed my glass on the bar and somewhat shakily asked for a refill. "No you've had enough cowboy, get yourself a taxi and go home." "How do I get a taxi?" She pointed to the wall on my right. "There's a free phone over there direct to the taxi company.

I managed to get to the phone, and with great difficulty grabbed the hand piece just as the wall was beginning to sway very gently from side to side. "Okay we'll send a taxi to you - be on the pavement outside."

Once outside I managed to steady the wall. The taxi pulled up and I plonked myself in the seat behind the driver. He twisted around. "Where to?" - good question. "I don't know, it's a motel." "Which motel?" - good question. "I don't know."

It was obvious the long suffering driver had plenty of experience of customers with limited brain power. "What does your motel look like?" - another good question. "I don't know." Then I had a brainwave. Digging into my pocket I fished out a slither of wood with a key attached. Having read the name of the motel he handed it back to me.

We drew up at a motel which through my blurred vision looked familiar. I settled up with the driver and made my way to my room, and as he drove away I could hear him roaring with laughter. It was obvious I'd made his day. With some degree of difficulty I managed to unlock my door. I fell onto the bed and passed out. A perfect day!

I flew out from Adelaide on 3rd August at ten twenty five and arrived in Alice at twelve twenty. I picked up some spares for the Toyotas and reached camp at seven o'clock.

The generator set had stopped and uncle Leslie couldn't get water to the onga pump - it was almost burned out. I finally got it going at nine o'clock and I went to bed.

It wasn't unusual for me to work on situations like this well after working hours, but I accepted it as part of the job.

Then came the northern territory holiday picnic day, when no-one worked. Everyone had left camp except for Harry and me. I made our breakfast, and when we finished he leaned back on his chair and told me a story. It was good to relax whilst the camp was quiet.

The next day we had a bad dust storm which lasted all day - too bad to work. It was so bad that I had to stop the generator, no point in clogging up the engine. All the vans were covered in sand both inside and out. Walking was near impossible as visibility was almost zero. We congregated in the cook house - it was the only place that was dust proof, and the tea urn worked overtime that day.

It was about that time or just after that we had a new mechanic, giving me more time with the men working on the road plant - but I was still very busy. The job was progressing well, but the terrain was becoming more and more difficult.

We had left the sandy area of the desert floor and were now entering an area covered in mulgar trees. Each root was as hard as iron and the Caterpillar 12e 17g grader wasn't heavy enough or powerful enough to cut through them efficiently. I mentioned this to Deb and suggested that we get a heavier grader. "Okay Robbie but you'll have to go and look things over before we commit ourselves to any deal. I trust your judgement."

She found a sales yard in Brisbane and another in Rockhampton. The machines looked promising, so on Monday 12th August I flew out of Alice with Ted heading for Brisbane via Sydney. We left at eleven o'clock, arriving in Sydney at two twenty - then leaving Sydney at three fifty we arrived in Brisbane at five o'clock. This was Ted's third flight and he handled it with no problem. I was really proud of him, but there was one little detail that I didn't share with him.

I always took my shoes off when flying as it was more comfortable. As we were nearing Sydney I noticed an unusual vibration coming through the floor, and the cabin staff weren't their usual happy selves - they were rushing about wearing worried expressions. I managed to catch the eye of one of the girls. Not wanting to cause a panic I just asked her how long it would be to Sydney. Her reply was "Twenty minutes." Thank god. The vibration was getting worse all the time. We landed safely in Sydney where the aircraft was immediately put out of commission - but not a word to

Ted. We moved onto another aircraft to finish the rest of our journey.

We were met in Brisbane by a tall slim guy in his late forties. He took us to the Acacia Ridge Motel. "I'll see you both after tea and give you the details concerning the sales yard for your visit tomorrow." With that he drove off. "Come on Ted, let's have a beer." The lounge was cool and comfortable. The beer went down without touching the sides and so did the second. Ted was relaxed and happy.

Not long after, and true to his word, our contact rolled up with our details. He was a nice outgoing sort of guy, but he made a big mistake - he told us that he was going to drink us under the table. I didn't make any comment, neither did Ted - but we had a good idea of what was going to happen.

It was late in the evening when we finished our last drink and our friend looked like he was going to pass out.

When he went to get up from the table his legs wouldn't work, but after about ten minutes we managed to get him as far as the door where he froze on the spot. Luckily some of his friends came to his rescue and took him home.

After breakfast Ted and I waited for him but he didn't show. So at nine o'clock we took a taxi to the sales yard. One of the salesmen took us round the machines. He must have thought we were stupid and tried to sell us some real crap - we were having none of it. "Leave us to it and if we see anything we'll come to the office and let you know."

We went from machine to machine, but nothing. Then we spotted a big old girl. A Caterpillar 16 grader - sitting covered in cobwebs up a corner. We started her up. No smoke or rattles. Her oil pressure was good. We went through the gears and operated the hydraulics - as good as gold - 225 horse power, length thirty one feet two inches, nine feet ten inches wide, eleven feet eight inches high, sixteen feet wide moleboard, two extra sets of cutting edges, weight twenty two tons. Serial number 49g1641. Seven thousand six hundred hours on the clock, fuel usage ten gallons per hour under hard working conditions.

She had been in two auctions but it appeared that no-one wanted her. Sales were looking for around forty five thousand dollars.

Transport was quoted at five thousand two hundred and fifty, but after a few arguments I got it down to four thousand. I also contacted the Cat.

Dealers and arranged for them to give it the once over to make sure everything was okay. I phoned Deb to tell her the price and suggested that she offered thirty eight thousand - even if they met her half way if would still be a good deal. She did, and she got a very good deal.

Around mid-day who should turn up but our friend and he looked real crook. He was full of apologies and worried that his boss would find out about the previous night's little error of judgement. He needn't have worried - Ted and I had no intention of talking to anyone about it!

We left Brisbane at seven o'clock the next morning arriving in Sydney at eight fifteen. Left Sydney at eight thirty and arrived in Alice at eleven twenty. Ted went to the office to see Deb, and I went via the bar in the airport to collect a Codan radio.

On the way back to camp we stayed at the Desert Oaks Earldunda for the night. We arrived at six o'clock just as the sun went down, both of us tired and happy, but my happiness wouldn't last for long.

Whilst we had been in Brisbane Tommy had gone off with the other Toyota, and when Colin wanted to go for some supplies he didn't turn up. The situation was bad. He didn't return with the vehicle until the day Ted and I were due back with the wages. He had been chasing emu through the mulgar trees and the tyres were full of punctures due to mulgar spikes being stuck in them.

It turned out that he had told lies about Billy burning perfectly good tyres to stop him using the Toyota. Billy should have told Deb what had really happened and kept the tyres for evidence. That was where the lack of man management skills led to his downfall. On looking back I realized that every time I mentioned Tommy's name to Deb all she would say is "I don't like that man." She told me that even in the early stages, and for no good reason, he had wanted me out of the job, but she was having none of it - good for her. He also tried to encourage the men to book days that weren't worked - he was beginning to show his true colours.

The day after we came back Ted looked really worried. Tommy had been boasting amongst the locals that he didn't like white men, and that he had already got rid of three and was going to get me.

He would tell me when Tommy was going to have me, and that I should tell him to 'fuck off' in front of all the men. He said they all liked me. I was shocked, it was the first time I'd ever heard Ted swear, but he was so annoyed.

I was put between a rock and a hard place. My job was to create a team of men to carry on with road construction after I had gone - it wasn't my policy to set man against man. I couldn't do that to Tommy, he would lose face with everyone even after I'd gone, and it would cause conflict amongst the men.

"Thanks for your support Ted but I can't do that - let me deal with it in my own way and don't worry." He walked quietly away. He didn't need to worry - I'd got the message and knew exactly what I would do.

It didn't take the mob long to start causing trouble. Jins (young women) and kids came into camp and congregated around my van, beating sticks on the door.

I was in the radio shack at the time and when they saw me they ran away. Later on I was having a cup of tea in the cook house when the jins came back, this time to the radio shack and began holding the emergency button for the flying doctor, shouting and whistling into the radio. They were unruly and completely out of control.

Soon after, a man in his early thirties walked into camp and demanded "You got meat?" "No." He gave me a dirty look and returned to one of the nearby humpies. Turned out he was Tommy's son-in-law.

When I saw Tommy three days later I asked him why the kids and young ones were causing trouble around the camp. He wouldn't look at me - he just walked away. 'Okay I understand' I thought to myself. 'You're such a coward you have to get others to do your dirty work, but it won't wash with me.'

Colin was on top form that day. As he was putting the roast beef from the oven onto the counter it fell onto the floor, which at the best of times resembled the well trodden area around a football goal post after a full season's matches.

After sliding it around the floor he picked it up by jamming a large carving knife and fork into it, at the same time saying to me "Look Robbie, untouched by human hand." He placed it on a large plate, carved it and served it onto the dinner plates.

Tommy asked me if I could sort out some summonses he had received from Adelaide. It appeared that someone had been using his name. I couldn't say 'no' because he was still one of the road gang and I was hoping things might calm down.

I went to borrow a slide projector from the headmaster at Indulkana school, and during our conversation he told me that two of the female teachers had hepatitis. That was a big worry.

One afternoon on my way back from Alice to the homeland, I stopped at the Desert Oaks Hotel. It was very quiet with no tourists that day, and there was only one person behind the bar - the cook. He was a likeable sort of guy in his mid forties, short and stocky, with hands like shovels, dark curly hair and a head like a water melon. "Hi Robbie what d ya want?" "A beer and a cheese sandwich please." He pulled me a beer and disappeared into the kitchen. After a couple of minutes he came back and squatted down facing me on the opposite side of the table. He held out a sandwich on a plate whilst staring at me intensely, not saying a word, but I noticed that he had both of his thumbs on the sandwich.

As I took it off him he drew back. Holding it up to my mouth I thought I detected movement, and as I took off the top layer of bread two bewildered eyes stared out at me. It was a live mouse! "You dirty fat little bastard, I'm gonna kill ya." I threw the sandwich at the swing door just as he was vanishing through it. I vaulted over the bar sending neatly stacked glasses flying and charged through the door, but was stopped in my tracks.

Not by the cook with a carving knife, but by the sight of him doubled up with one hand on the work surface and the other holding his chest. He was screaming with laughter and tears were running down his face. What could I do? I intended to put a few dents in him, but instead I saw the funny side of it and joined him in a good laugh. After a few beers I waved him goodbye. He was still laughing as I drove off.

An hour later I pulled in at the Hotel in Kulgera and ordered a beer and a cheese sandwich. When it arrived the barman gave me a puzzled look as I opened it up to look inside (no mouse.)

We moved to camp site number five and during the evening a car drew up near the camp. They pelted my van until the early hours then drove off, but I said nothing to the men - I didn't want to get them involved in my problems.

After tea one evening I was disconnecting the water pipe from the back of the tanker. The clutch had gone and we were going to take it by low loader to Alice the next day for repair. As I put the spanner onto the nut some instinct told me to turn around. As I did so, a man with glazed eyes as though in a dream strode slowly and purposefully towards me. In his right hand he held a nula nula high above his head - it was obvious he was heading for me.

Okay, a quick estimate, he was about five paces from me. I would have to step back about three paces to get out of the soft sand for a good footing. He was advertising where the blow was going to come from which made it easier for me to deal with. I had attended karate classes for two years back in the UK so I had a clear picture of what was going to happen, but I didn't expect what happened next.

Okay, three steps backwards took me to solid ground, and I felt a bit happier knowing what I must do. I didn't take my eyes off his - I wanted him to get near enough for me to get under the blow by blocking it with two hands, then twist to my right and come back hard. By driving my left elbow into his ribs I could break two or possibly three - enough to put him out of action. I was waiting to see the reflex in his eyes then I would strike fast and hard. Three paces, then two, one more and I would have the bastard.

Suddenly instead of looking at the man I was staring at the back of a head. The man had stopped in his tracks just as I was prepared to go in, and he was still holding the nula nula above his head. The man who had stood in between us at the last second was uncle Leslie. Face to face he screamed at the man in aboriginal. Very slowly he began to lower his nula nula. Uncle was still screaming at him.

He very slowly lowered his head, turned around and walked away. Until he was out of sight uncle wouldn't budge, then he returned to his camp fire nearby and his kunga, my aunt Mona. I watched him sit down as though nothing had happened.

I didn't realise at the time he must have seen the man approaching me and moved pretty quickly to stop him. My instinct was to go over to this brave man and thank him, but there are no such words in the aboriginal language as 'thankyou' or 'please' - so I carried on disconnecting the water pipe in readiness for the trip to Alice.

The next day turned out to be a very sad one. Around mid-day uncle Leslie returned to camp in his four wheeled drive. With him were my tribal brother Billy and my aunt Mona. Uncle got out and walked over to me, and without saying a word squeezed my hand and hugged me. He gave me a long look, turned around, got into his vehicle and drove away. I couldn't take my eyes off him. I watched as he disappeared from sight. I watched the dust trail as he headed east along our newly constructed road. Then it hit me - that was the last time I would ever see him - and I was devastated.

The reason he had to go was that he and his family were now in danger of payback from the mob - this would result in a member of his family being murdered. A few years later Billy was murdered on the homeland. It broke uncle's heart and he took it to his grave.

Now it was time for me to confront Tommy. After tea I waited for him to come down the steps from the cook house and stood directly in his path. "What's wrong with you Tommy, tell me what I've done to you?" He wouldn't answer and went to walk away. Again I blocked his path. "Come on out with it." He looked down at the floor and tried to walk away again. By then I was losing my temper, the matter was serious. "Come on, fight it out here and now, man to man." He began to mutter, and in between mumbling he said "I won't do it here, I do it black fella way." He was a real coward.

He still remained in his humpy on a hill behind the camp. In the afternoon whilst the men were working, his son-in-law came into camp demanding kooka. Once again I told him the food was for the road gang. He glared at me and returned to his humpy, produced a 303 rifle, took aim, and shot it over my head.

I was startled, but then I composed myself - those guys could shoot the head off a match at twenty yards. If he'd wanted to kill me he could have done, but there would have been payback by the men and he knew it.

When they came back to camp I told them of the incident. They said nothing to me, but went up to his humpy where I heard raised voices. By the next morning the man had gone, but Tommy wasn't finished with me.

That night after I had switched off the generator set, two four wheeled drives came labouring up to his camp. Whatever they were carrying they were loaded. The dogs began to bark in his camp and everything was quiet. A short while later I heard the children crying which was most unusual.

By now it was dark and sensing something was wrong I took my swag into the cook house. My instinct was right - I was about to encounter a fierce witch doctor and his mob. It turned out that he would visit me quite a few times after dark when I was alone. They would throw small stones at the front and rear of my van which would go on until early morning. I was told that they would hunt me down and I would be glad to go - but they didn't bargain on me being an obstinate little bastard. I had a job to do and I would do my best to complete it.

Ted and I had returned from the road gang on 25th and went for a coffee in the cook house. Colin was on his usual form (bless him.) He removed an object from the oven - it was as big as a football and as black as a burned out meteorite. Whilst jabbing it with a fork he exclaimed "Beautiful!" Just how we all survived his offerings I'll never know!

One day when the men were heading for their evening meal, I decided to go back a few kilometres down the road to check on a couple of low spots that had been stoned up to road level. After checking it out I drove off-road to a small hill. I left my Toyota about fifty yards away, and walked through the soft sand to the hill. I climbed up and got a very good view of the surrounding desert. What a view - it seemed to go on forever. Just how anyone could survive out there was nothing short of a miracle.

After a few minutes I decided to go back to camp. On my way down I got my foot jammed in the rough rocky surface, twisting my ankle badly. It was all I could do to get down to the bottom, mainly sliding on my bum. I tried to hobble through the sand to my vehicle, but I was in so much pain that I had to crawl.

I hadn't told anyone where I was going so it was quite possible no-one would miss me - and there was another problem - 'how the hell am I going to drive with only one good foot.' As I looked towards my Toyota I could see a dust trail approaching. The vehicle stopped next to mine and a skinny figure got out. It was Harry!

He came over and helped me to my feet but I couldn't move, so the big fella scooped me up like a baby and deposited me at the door of the Toyota. "It's no good Harry, you have to take me back in yours. How did you know I was here?" He wouldn't answer. It turned out that he was concerned at not seeing me at tea, and came looking for me. It wouldn't be the last time Harry would come to my rescue - but the next time he would save my life.

We had bad dust storms and high winds one night. The temperature was twenty five degrees and everyone had very little sleep. By midnight it had cooled off a little but the dust was still getting everywhere. During the day I took the men to see the doctor at Mimili for hepatitis tests - we were all worried about the outcome.

Whilst all the nightly stoning had been going on I still had Tommy on the road team under my instruction. We carried on as though nothing had happened because no way was I going to break up the men.

Deb had fiddled two days off for me at the end of August to see the Henley on Todd river regatta in Alice. She was good like that. If there was an event going on she would find some excuse to get me up there. As I said, we knew each other well, like an old married couple. "Got you two days at the Desert Rose Rob." That was when she told me about the regatta. So there I was.

At eight thirty the parade of boats went up the mall carried by their crews, towards the river at the top of the town. There were dinghies, life boats, rowing boats, sail boats, and a paddle steamer that was already moored along the river bank. The races began at eleven fifteen. There were crowds of onlookers lining both sides of the river and big burly lifeguards on patrol.

It was a colourful sight with all the different sails and brightly coloured boats. At one point some children went very close to the edge but were ushered back by the lifeguards. It was a great day out for everyone with lots of excitement. Oh, and I forgot to mention - the river Todd was as dry as dust!! One year it had flooded and the regatta looked like being cancelled, until someone got a bull dozer and bull dozed a spot high up above the water line.

You see, a river with water in it is no good for bottomless leg-powered boats! I wouldn't have missed it for the world.

At one fifteen I was getting a bit thirsty so I headed back into Alice and to the front bar of the black fella pub, the Stuart Arms, where I got chatting to some of the locals. They were a great bunch of characters and I felt really at ease, swapping stories and telling them how the road from Indulkana to Mimili was progressing.

As we were talking a young fella got up and fed the juke box a couple of coins, and when it started to play he shouted "Dig that crazy rock and roll man" and began to dance. The thing was, he was doing a lizard dance and he had everyone in stitches (great entertainment.) His antics reminded me of a story that uncle Leslie had told me about the little lizard man.

'There was a little man called Linga who lived in a place near what is now called Uluru. He made a boomerang which was very special to him. He carefully shaped it and after many days he threw it to see if it would return to him. It went higher and higher then fell to earth a short distance away burying itself, and it created a big hill of sand.

He looked everywhere for it but with no success. He was so desperate to get it back that he dug the ground with his bare hands, digging holes and gullies, and Uluru was formed.

Linga died not long after, and his spirit was so upset that it turned him into a sand lizard. If you're quiet and careful you'll see him today still digging small sand hills - still looking for that boomerang.'

People still do the lizard dance, as that young man did in the Stuart Arms.

Early in September Teddy was looking really worried. Hepatitis was rampant in the area and his little daughter was suffering symptoms. He was waiting for test results to come through from Alice. If they were positive he would have to take two or three weeks off work to stay with her. "Take as long as you need Ted and don't worry about your job, it'll still be here for you. Good luck with your little girl. Are you okay for diesel?"

He checked the fuel gauge. "I could do with half a tank to top her up." With that he drove over to the bowser, fuelled up and left camp.

I saw a dust cloud go past the camp heading east towards Indulkana. It was the TAFE guy. He was supposed to call in once a month to see how things were progressing and to collect my weekly report sheets. He only stopped once, and that was at the meeting concerning young Billy and the tyres. He had no intention of calling in at camp to see me but he did call in towards the end of the job, and uncle Leslie's words would echo "Always talk to the snake's head, not its tail."

After dark someone began throwing small stones at the back of my van. They had woken me up at three o'clock during the previous night doing the same thing. It was beginning to make me feel tired but I wouldn't give in to them, no way.

It was a national aboriginal holiday on 11th September and I was the only one in camp. Early morning, three thirty, I had taken a borrowed rifle and shot a rabbit for breakfast. There was a young dingo by the rabbit burrows waiting for a meal. Although he was in range I wouldn't shoot the little fella - he was just as hungry as I was. 'Live and let live' that's my motto.

At two thirty that afternoon I arrived at the YWCA where Deb had me booked in for two nights, due to the fact that the Desert Rose and the Anglican Lodge were fully booked. It cost thirty eight dollars a night and six dollar fifty cents for breakfast. They also served lunch and an evening meal. It was very good quality - and yes - you read it right first time - Young Women's Christian Association. It was the only place where Deb could get me fixed up, and under the sex discrimination act they couldn't refuse. It was full of young female tourists from all over the world. They were very interested in me and asked lots of questions.

My bedroom was at the top of the stairs near reception so I was able to get an early shower and start the day without waking anyone. At first I was embarrassed - being a rough arsed old bushie with shirt and shorts, sticky with sweat and dust, and an overnight bag - but once I was cleaned up I felt much better. Those two days were very enjoyable.

By that time Teddy was learning to make decisions for himself regarding the running of the camp, and the daily machine allocation for the men. I was really proud of him.

Back at camp the stoning continued and someone tried my door handle during the night. The door was unlocked so they could've come in, but they didn't. It was all designed to scare me but it didn't work.

I had a country and western tape which I played, and by the time it had finished whoever was doing the throwing was fast asleep under my van snoring his head off.

It was 'look after camp day' and I started the generator set at five minutes to seven. We kept it turned off at night to save fuel - also it wasn't the snake season so we didn't need the lights on after dark. I had a light breakfast, cheese on toast, grapefruit, and a cup of tea - and did some washing, towels, overalls, shirts, socks, and jocks.

The youths were still running out of control around camp. Everyone was using the camp radio, shouting and yelling. The white Toyota was taken from camp to who knew where. I would be glad to get some peace and quiet. Tommy was really causing me trouble - all the more reason for me to dig my heels in. As I said, I could be an awkward little bastard, no problem.

I had to go to Mimili to arrange for the collection of a tanker full of water for the cook house and the ablutions van. I was glad to get away from all the noise and youths charging around everywhere like mad things. I left camp number five and headed west towards Mimili. It's a funny thing but I was beginning to think like an aboriginal, and even the slightest wheel tracks told a story - and so it was that I spotted a very faint set of tracks headed south off the Mimili road. My curiosity got the better of me and I followed the almost invisible marks for maybe thirty minutes, until I came across something that I never expected to see so far into the desert.

I parked my Toyota in the shade of a giant gum tree, got out and took in the view. It was a small green flat valley, about five hundred yards long by two hundred yards wide. All around its perimeter were large healthy gum trees. The centre was covered in deep luscious vegetation dotted with shallow fresh pools, and a short distance to my right were a family of kangaroos lying in the shade licking their coats as though I wasn't there.

At that moment a station wagon drew up by my side - it was one of the road team, Peter. He looked very annoyed. "Robbie what are you doing here?" Taken by surprise I bleated out "Just admiring the view." Before I could say anything else he pointed back the way I had come. "I think you'd better go that way." Then without another word he turned his vehicle and drove off at speed.

Suddenly it dawned on me - I was on a sacred site and I could have been expelled from the homeland, because although I was adopted by the tribe I was an uninitiated man, therefore not allowed there.

Peter didn't say anything to the men about the incident - he made allowances. Like uncle Leslie had said "Don't be too hard on Robbie, he's only an ignorant little white fella." I arrived in Mimili about half an hour later and was told that we would have to wait two days for the water, due to the fact that the water pump had broken down.

The next day a new generator set arrived. Young Jimmy helped me off-load it and we gave it a good check over - oil, air filter, battery, water system, loose nuts, screws etc. We bled the fuel system and ran it off-load for thirty minutes.

I then went up the road to see how the men were progressing, only to find that someone had thrown debris and a car bonnet onto the newly constructed road.

That night the stoning began at three o'clock and continued until daybreak. I could hear young male voices south of the camp. At day break I went to check on the area and saw the gina (tracks) of the same person who had placed the car bonnet on the road. I took Harry to see them and his comment was "One of Tommy's sons, silly young man." Over the next couple of days the stoning at night continued and I was tired through lack of sleep, but they would have to do better than that if they wanted to drive me out.

I put Tommy on the D6 dozer pushing trees, but we needed a machine with an angle blade. The mulgar was becoming dense so I did a deal with Mimili. We would repair and grade their airstrip in exchange for the use of their dozer with an angle blade.

The men developed a way of driving a straight road through the mulgar trees by first walking through on foot. After a couple of kilometres they would set fire to a few rubber tyres. The smoke would rise and the dozers and graders would head for it - and you know what? - it worked perfectly every time!

One afternoon Sandy and I were on part of the old road deciding if we should re-build it or construct a new section of road to by-pass it. The area was flat littered with rocks, deep loose sand and dead tree stumps. He pointed to a rock shaped like a dome around twenty feet in diameter.

Its centre was around two feet above ground level and its outer edges disappeared into the ground.

At its centre lay a flat stone roughly the size of a roofing tile. He dropped to one knee and removed the stone to reveal a hole just big enough to put a hand down. He indicated for me to put my hand in. "No way Sandy."

He laughed and said "Look Robbie" and plunged his hand in almost to his elbow. I had no idea of just what was going to happen, but I needn't have worried. As he lifted his hand out of the hole water dripped off his fingers. He explained to me that it was an ancient water hole. In olden times anangu would walk from one to another. If one was dry they walked to the next, and if that was dry they would die. The amazing thing was that to find it was like looking for a needle in a haystack. A person could walk over it and not know it was there.

I was treated as one of the anangu and I considered it a privilege to be taken into their confidence. I was shown things that no other white fella living on the homeland knew about, and the more I learned about the people the more I admired and respected them. I was indeed a lucky little white fella.

One afternoon on one of my many trips to and from Alice, I had left Kulgera heading south towards Indulkana on the rough unmade road. There was a brand new car parked up with a small box-type trailer in tow. The trailer was obviously too frail for the outback conditions and the axle had broken in two.

The occupants were in trouble so I stopped and spoke to the driver. It was obvious he hadn't got a clue what to do, it turned out he was a city dweller. His wife was sitting alongside him as quiet as a mouse. The temperature was in the high 40s, but as luck would have it he had plenty of fuel so could keep the air conditioning on, giving them some degree of comfort.

On closer inspection I could see that the axle was repairable. "Do you want me to go back to Kulgera and send a guy with welding gear to you? I don't advise you to go yourself leaving the trailer here. Although there's very little traffic using this road you might find your gear missing when you get back. What do you think?" He hummed and hahhed and didn't even discuss it with his wife.

At this point he seemed to be a bit of a know-it-all, and had he been on his own I would have left him to stew in his own juice, but I felt sorry for his wife. Just then I caught sight of two little blonde headed boys who looked to be and four and six years old, playing in the hot sun about forty metres away in the bush (what an idiot.) "Get those boys in the shade." He just ignored me, and by now I was beginning to lose my patience with him. I called them over. "What's that you've got boys?" They produced what looked like apples with the colours of a cucumber and fine hairs sticking out of them.

It was a plant that grew at ground level, much like a cucumber plant. What they had in their hands was highly toxic and could kill if eaten. He was letting the boys play in the heat of the desert, and besides sunstroke they could have been poisoned. "Get those boys into some shade and don't let them pick up anything you know nothing about." Reluctantly he called them into the car.

"Okay I'll go and get someone to come out to you. It took me an hour to get to Kulgera. The repair guy would start out in a couple of minutes with his mobile welder and not be far behind me. Another hour later I reached the car and the broken down trailer. I stopped and told the guy what was going on then went on my way. A short distance down the road I saw the boys, with red faces, still playing out in the sun and thought to myself 'I'm glad that stupid bastard isn't my dad.'

Bob's watch. (A yarn from one of the regulars in the Stuart Arms.) Bob was fencing at Beltana station in the Flinders Ranges north of Adelaide. He had a pocket watch in a pouch on his belt and while he was boring a post hole it dropped out. Later in the afternoon he reached for the pouch - no watch. He said "Stuff it, I'll get it when I'm running the wires through in a couple of days" but he didn't find it.

Four years later the wires had become fairly slack on the fence and Bob came back to dog up the strainer posts. Whilst he was doing this he found his watch. It was still ticking and tightly wound and it showed the correct time. Of course we asked "How come Bob?" He said "It was just luck - when it fell it settled on top of a snake hole, and when the snake went in and out he kept it wound up for me!"

The men had worked well considering some of them had never had a job that was so demanding - some had never experienced the rigid hours and continual ten days on and four days off. They were getting tired and I understood their feelings. To date they had done well and I was proud of them, so it was no surprise when I was invited to their meeting in camp to discuss their idea of having the next ten days off without pay. They had worked nine months, that's a long time for the anangu. I told them that I was going for my R and R on 26th September, and that TAFE didn't control the anangu in the road gang. I also had worked a lot of days overtime unpaid. Teddy and the Executive agreed that the men should indeed have those days off.

Early in the job I had met man, forty years old, raking the gravel level in the school yard at Indulkana. While we were talking I spotted his young German Shepherd lying nearby.

He wouldn't take his eyes off his master - it was plain to see they bonded well. "What about selling me your dog" I asked him. "No way." "Why not?" "You never know when somebody might want to sneak up on a fella." It turned out that he was on parole. He'd committed one murder in Oodnadatta and another in Cooberpede. Tommy told me that he wasn't allowed in either of those places - he was going to be dealt with in the anangu way (murdered.) As soon as the people found out where he was they would do it their way and in their time. His body would go to Wyalla and it would be classed as tribal fighting - nothing would be said.

The day before I was due to get the coach at Indulkana I found I had run out of cash - 'oh shit.' What the hell was I going to do for grog on the trip to Melbourne. I put the word on the men but to no avail. Then I spotted Harry. Some time ago I had given him twenty dollars when he was broke, maybe he would give me good payback. He signalled me to his sleeping van then gave me a sign to stop - a clenched fist in a downward motion as though thumping some invisible table. I could hear him searching in the van and a couple of minutes later he ambled across to me with a big grin on his face and stuffed a twenty dollar bill into my hand. The big fella had saved my day. "Thanks Harry."

I couldn't sleep that night. It was one of those times where I kept turning things over and over in my mind. I just couldn't understand why Tommy was so hostile whilst the rest of the men were so protective towards me. Every time he had come to me with any personal problems I made time to help him. Like the time one of his daughters was kidnapped by an aboriginal man.

His kunga was beside herself with grief. "Robbie would you write a letter for me to the police in Alice Springs to get my daughter back?" I did as she asked and posted it at the post office in Indulkana.

On our drive back to camp Teddy told me "The police won't do anything, it's a tribal dispute. Maybe in a year's time he'll return her to the family, perhaps with a wee eye (baby) or pregnant. There'll be lots of shouting, things will quieten down, and it will be accepted into the family - that's what normally happens." However she returned to camp two months later after escaping from him. It turned out that this was the same man who some time earlier had come into camp demanding kooka (meat) - the same man that shot a 303 rifle over my head.

The next day Teddy drove me to Indulkana and waited with me until the coach arrived to take me on my R and R. He shook my hand before I boarded. "Don't forget Robbie, travel in their time not your own." "I will."

With that I found myself a seat and settled down for the bumpy journey to Adelaide. After a while I began to feel tired but I was unable to sleep. The journey seemed to go on forever. The endless stoning of my van at night was beginning to take its toll.

When I eventually arrived in Adelaide I was told that there was over a seven hour wait for the connecting coach for Melbourne later that day. I desperately needed to find somewhere to stay for the night and get the coach next day. Twenty dollars was all I had - that would buy my grog but not a motel room.

Reaching into my pocket I dug out my tattered note book. Inside was a phone number and an address in Hyde Park, a very posh area of Adelaide. This had been given to me by the American exchange school teacher whom I met on a coach journey from Alice to Indulkana a couple of months earlier. We chatted and got on well, and she gave me her details saying that I should look her up some time when I was in Adelaide. Well now seemed as good a time as any, so I rang the number. Luckily for me she was at home and I explained my situation. "No problem Robbie, get yourself down here. I have to go out now but I'll leave the key under the door mat. There's food in the fridge, help yourself. I'll see you later and when I get back we'll have a talk. By the way there's a cycle in the shed if you fancy a ride around Adelaide, but watch out for the tram tracks."

The taxi dropped me off outside a large two-storey red brick house. The whole area looked as though it had been developed in the early nineteen thirties, very upper class and posh. Once inside I made myself a light meal, then went into the shed.

With the key safely under the mat I took a ride into Adelaide. It was very busy, and she was right about the tram tracks. After a while I'd had enough and returned to the house.

Wandering upstairs I found the bathroom. It was beautifully tiled. There was a large free-standing cast iron bath with a rolled top standing in the centre of the room with hot and cold water. I was in heaven. I left my dusty gear on the floor, ran the bath almost full, and had a good soak. It was so relaxing, just what I needed. I was in there so long my skin began to wrinkle - 'better get out and dry off.' I changed into some clean clothes courtesy of my overnight bag, and felt like a new man.

The phone rang - it was her. "I won't be home until late. There are some chocolates on the bedside table, and a big television at the foot of the bed. Make yourself at home and I'll see you later."

I felt guilty dropping in on her like this, but she was okay about it. The bed was an enormous double. I stripped naked, got into bed, switched on the television and fell fast asleep, only to be woken up by the ringing of the telephone. It was a man's voice asking if she was there. "No" I answered. "Okay see her tomorrow." With that he rang off.

Still half asleep I gazed around the room. Near the large window was a three-mirror dressing table. Next to that was a chair with a set of lady's silk pyjamas draped over it. What the hell was I playing at, naked in a woman's bed? It wasn't fair to her or to Cathie. Picking up my clothes I walked down the landing, found a room with a single bed, and crashed there for the night.

I awoke the next morning to the smell of cooking. I got dressed and went down to the kitchen where she was preparing breakfast, and I apologised for not being awake when she got home. She was okay about it and wasn't phased at all. We talked for a couple of hours, then it was time to get a taxi and head for the coach depot. We became good friends and were happy in each other's company. That's what life's all about.

Before I caught the coach to Melbourne I phoned Cathie to give her my arrival time, in order that she could meet me at the station. Once again the journey seemed never ending, and I was feeling really rat shit. I was so happy to see her smiling face and to get the big lick treatment off Sally even though she had a tongue as rough as a blacksmith's file.

Once in the house I began to unpack my gear. Cathie took my arm, "Are you okay?" "Yes, just a bit tired that's all." She frowned, "You don't look okay."

It was a fact, I wasn't okay but I didn't want to burden her with my problems.

She said "I've got a couple of jobs for you to do around the house but I'll tell you about them after you've had some sleep." It was obvious she suspected something was wrong. "Okay I'll go and get my head down for a few minutes." Six hours later she woke me up with a cup of tea. She looked really worried. "You shouted 'leave me alone' - you were having a nightmare. What's going on?"

Reluctantly I told her everything, after all she deserved an honest answer. At first she went quiet then she let rip. "Don't go back there, I don't want you to be treated like that." "I have to." "No you don't!" She stared hard at me. "I have a commitment to the men and to TAFE - I must." The stare gave way to a look of anger. "Well I don't want you to." To change the subject I walked into the garden. "Back of the house could do with a lick of paint, have you got any?" "Yes it's under the porch."

Over the next couple of days I kept myself busy with the paint brush, and to her credit she didn't pursue the matter any further.

Gradually I began to feel less tired and more like my old self. "Don't fret Cathie, I promise you I'll be okay - only three months to the end of my contract." The last thing I wanted to do was to upset her, but I knew deep down that she would worry. The time flew by, and after saying our 'goodbye's I began my journey back to the homeland, wondering what was in store for me.

After stepping off the coach at Indulkana I waited for my lift back to camp. It never came. Turned out Tommy was supposed to pick me up but it looked like he was up to his old tricks again. That night I stayed with a friend and his family who lived nearby. He was the TAFE teacher at the local school. Teddy must have realised what had happened and next morning at nine o'clock he came fetch me. "Robbie I've got some bad news for you, the witch doctor, your friend, is dead." I didn't want to believe it.

He had saved my life when I had chemical poisoning. What a shock to come back to. "Take me to his grave." Ted drove me down to the graveyard, and there on the outer edge he pointed to a new grave. "That's it." I dropped to my knees and sobbed my heart out - this was one of the saddest days of my life.

As I got back into the Toyota Ted had a question for me. "Robbie did you take any photos of him?" "Yes" I replied, "But a strange thing happened, they turned out to be blank negatives of him - the only blanks in my camera." He looked relieved. "That's okay Robbie, if they had turned out I would have had to ask you for them and would have destroyed them, that's the anangu way."

Then he told me that the witch doctor's name would never be mentioned again, and anyone coming onto the homeland with that name would be called Kuminara - and if a creek had been named after him it would be called Kuminara Creek.

As we were driving I reflected on an incident which happened back in camp 5 while uncle Leslie was still there. It was early in the morning. The humpies near the camp were deserted, no children playing, nothing. Everyone had moved onto a new hunting ground, building new humpies. I was alone watching the camp. Nothing for it but to grab a cup of tea in the cook house and relax before checking the generator set for fuel, and filling in my weekly report.

As I gazed through the window something caught my eye. Sitting motionless at the entrance of one of the humpies was a frail old lady.

Her grey hair was tied neatly back - her face showed no emotion. She was just sitting there staring out across the valley.

Two huntsmen came along the side of the hill and sat down facing her. One gave her a plastic bottle which looked like it contained water. The other gave her a small parcel of food. After a few minutes they got up and left. She touched the bottle and she touched the small parcel of food, then she dropped her hands down by her side but made no attempt to eat or drink - she just sat there looking across the valley. She seemed calm and at peace.

At ten o'clock I returned to the cook house to make a sandwich and a cup of tea. Looking out of the window I saw that the old lady was still sitting there staring across the valley. The sun was beginning to come around to the front of the humpy, and my instinct was to get a sheet off my bed and drape it near to her to give her some shade, but I dared not.

Evening came and she was still sitting there. Once more the hunters came and sat down in front of her and spoke quietly to her, then they got up and left.

What was going through her mind as she sat there? She was someone's daughter, sister, lover, mother, grandmother. What was going through her mind? The old lady was dying but she was doing it the way it had been done for hundreds if not thousands of years. She was at peace and dying with dignity.

The next morning I had to leave early for Alice. On my return three days later the humpy was empty. I asked uncle Leslie if she had died. He replied "Owa." Then I asked if she was buried Tribal way or Christian way. He just gave me a look. I knew the answer.

When Colin and I were having a drink one day in the front bar of the Stuart Arms in Alice he told me a story. 'Back in April 1968 whilst driving past Mount Freeling airstrip his passenger said "Go back, I've seen a snake." He didn't believe him but decided to go back approximately half a mile. He stopped and said "Snake my arse." The passenger said "A bit further" so he drove back a bit further.

They found a python looking similar to a big tyre on the airstrip, at least eighteen feet in length with an eight inch spine on the end of his tail which he used to attract birds.

They stoned him and killed him. It took the two of them to pick him up and put him in the back of the Falcon ute. His head was at least four inches across.

They drove another two hours west and arrived at the Lyndhurst pub situated north of Leigh Creek on the junction of the Birdsville and Strazleki track. The Lyndhurst was a single storey, weather beaten shack with a rusty tin roof and just enough room for a bar and a store room.

The owner and bar keeper was a well known character in the bush. He was in his fifties, and had spent most of his life in the bush. They had a few drinks and the conversation turned to snakes. Of course the bar keeper could never be beaten by anything when it came to conversation. He'd had snakes as long as his bar, and he was really ranting and raving about snakes - he couldn't get off the subject.

After about an hour, while he was attending to other business behind the bar, Colin said to his passenger "Go out to the ute and drag that snake in around the bottom of the bar." The snake still had nerves in him because he had only died three hours earlier.

The bar keeper turned to serve them. "Another drink?" Colin asked him if he'd ever seen a big snake. "Yes" he said "I've seen them up to eighteen feet long. Colin said "Come out from behind the bar and look at this one." He just laughed. "Don't laugh, come out and have a look." He came out and looked on the floor of the bar, went as white as milk and fainted. They brought him round in a couple of seconds, and he said "Well you've done me - you can drink on me for the rest of the afternoon."

At seven o'clock just gone dark they were about to leave, when he said to them "Would you leave that snake with me, I want to make some belts out of the skin?" Colin said "Definitely not, this snake comes with us." They were going about another hundred miles north to Marree, a fairly large aboriginal camp where Colin knew several people. He would like to give it to them for tucker because a snake that large in that part of the country was a delicacy.

So two and a half hours after leaving the pub Colin, passenger and snake arrived at Marree. The people got a big fire going - they chopped off the snake's head and put him on the coals in the fire. Then the dancing started. Colin and his passenger stayed the night and the dancing continued all night.'

I knew the Lyndhurst well and it was just as Colin described it. I'd called in there when I worked for Blackwood Hodge on my visits to various talcum quarries in South Australia. As a matter of fact I had travelled quite a fair bit in South Australia, from the Barrosa Valley famous for its wine, to Wilpeena Pound, a large hole in the landscape believed to have been formed by the impact of a giant meteorite millions of years ago.

While Colin was telling me this story there was an elderly aboriginal lady sitting nearby with a younger one. She said to her "Do you know that fella?" pointing to Colin. She replied "No." The older one then said "Do you remember that big snake in Marree?" "Yes but I was only a little girl then." She told her "That's the fella that bin bring him." They then bought Colin several beers. The young woman was only three years old when Colin took the snake to Marree and she could remember that, but obviously not Colin.

On my way back from R and R I met Deb in the Grosvenor Hotel in Adelaide. She was down there on a short break. It was pure luck that I bumped into her, and we enjoyed a whiskey or two together. She said "When you get back and are sorted I want you to come up to Alice and see me in the office. There are a couple of details I want you to sort out."

After a nice meal with her it was time for me to catch the coach. As she waved me off I couldn't believe how we bumped into each other - it was pure coincidence - Australia is such a large country but sometimes it seems so small.

Previously, when I'd heard of the witch doctor's death, I also found out that we had a gudarchi man in camp. When I got back to camp the men were very quiet. It was unusual for them to be like this and I was determined to get to the bottom of it. Peter was sitting on his own in the cook house with a cup of tea in his hand. It was obvious that he was worried about something.

"What's wrong Pete?" "Last night after dark there was a big explosion outside the camp and the road was on fire. All the dogs were barking, and everyone was shouting to drive the gudarchi man away. Tommy let off lots of bangs, and everyone went into the cook house. No-one went to bed until late, and they all slept with their lights on." I was surprised that the men didn't desert the camp - it was to their credit they didn't. "What about gina?" (tracks) I asked Peter. His reply was instant "No gina."

It was getting late in the evening and I was ready for bed - 'what's going to happen tonight?' I thought. Nothing did happen.

The next morning the men carried on with the road construction, but it was plain to see they were all still shaken from the incident. By the evening I had forgotten about it, that was until I was almost in camp.

To my left I saw a shape, the outline of a man - but there was something about it that wasn't quite right. As I turned into camp it disappeared from sight. As I drove in the first person I came across was Tommy, and after describing to him what I had seen he grabbed his rifle. "Come on Robbie, show me."

We walked along to where the shape had disappeared but there were no human gina, there were only the tracks of a dog. Tommy looked at the tracks and turned to me. I had never seen him so worried. "That's how the gudarchi man travels, he leaves no human gina."

One day on my way to Mimili to get cabi (water) there was a group of about seven or eight women sitting in a circle near the road. Amongst them was a white woman about thirty years old. She was an anthropologist. I recognised her from a meeting a couple of weeks earlier.

She shouted "Hi Robbie how are you?" Not wanting to appear ignorant I stopped to talk to her. I didn't know it then, but the women had something planned for me. Their ages ranged from late teens to maybe thirty or forty. They were happy and laughing, and talking away in aboriginal.

They got to their feet, took off their tops and began to sing, and as they sang they moved forwards and backward in a little dance towards the centre of the circle. Some of them were studying my face and with good reason! The white woman took off her top and joined them and as they moved into the centre of the circle they pushed up their breasts (no bras.) I didn't expect that.

I stood there for a few minutes taking it all in. There were big tits, little tits, all sorts of shapes and sizes. Then they sat down and began chatting amongst themselves again. Show over, I thanked the ladies and carried on into Mimili.

Whilst I was pumping the water into one of our tanks Ted came over to me. "Palya Robbie." "Palya Ted how are you?" "Not good Robbie. I've got to take number one wife to Adelaide for an operation. Will you tell Teddy I'm finishing, and could you tell him I want my holiday pay and wages as soon as possible?" It wasn't a problem, but it meant that I would have to scout around for his replacement pretty quick.

At seven in the evening Colin took the white Toyota to Granite Downs for some meat. He didn't need a driving licence because the homeland was under the control of the anangu - no licence required. All he had to do was to cross the Stuart highway and he was on private property about seventy kilometres from camp.

On the way there he asked Teddy for some cabi out of the long range tank of his Toyota. He returned at eight thirty without the meat. He nearly blacked out - it took him five minutes to get around the Toyota to get cabi out of the tank, then he made it to bed. He was really crook, poor old Col. Next day the cook was a skinny little white fella - me.

It turned out that he'd picked up some kind of bug. Teddy suspected he'd been eating some of his own cooking! The following morning he was still crook but getting better. In the evening he was feeling well enough to go again to Granite Downs for the meat. He took his kunga with him and they got back at seven o'clock - with the meat.

Remembering what Deb had said to me in Adelaide, I went in to Alice to see her. "What do you want to see me about Deb?" She began to smile. "Do you want a drink Robbie?" "Yes please." She made me a cup of tea - it was terrible, tasted like salt water. That was the trouble with Alice, all the water came from a bore hole and it was saline. When we returned to the homeland the water was different again, resulting in a bad stomach and the runs. That's why everyone drank beer.

"I want you to tell me what plant we really need for next year Robbie." "That's easy Deb, all you need is maybe a multi-tiered self-propelled roller and another tip truck - and better access to water! The rest of your plant is okay and once you get past Mimili you won't need to use their bull dozer, the two graders will cope." "That was all I needed to hear thanks Robbie."

Now back to the road programme. Teddy had cut a beautiful straight road, but one spot was allowed to creep about four feet into the carriageway causing an unsightly kink on the north side of the road. "Are you going to cut that piece straight Ted?" The answer was a simple "No." I couldn't understand it - the road had a bend in it but what was the reason?

"Robbie you see that small tree in the centre of the kink? Well one day it may save someone's life, may even be yours. If you broke down that's the only shade around here." Looking around, he was right. Although only a small tree about ten feet high, there was no other shade as far as the eye could see. Once again I was being educated into the aboriginal way of thinking.

A young man came into camp one day with a scald on his left arm and part of his torso. He was accompanied by two young friends. They'd been playing up at Marla Bore and the police chased them onto the homeland. They were driving an old Holden saloon and by the time they got near to us the radiator had begun to boil. Stopping at an ancient water hole near to our camp, which we knew nothing about, he opened the bonnet and was scalded when the top radiator hose blew. They were in real trouble. Colin and I were the only ones in camp. I radioed the flying doctor, but there was no answer. Colin smothered his arm with butter and wrapped it in kitchen foil. (I thought he would put it in the oven and cook it - ha ha.) I asked them if they wanted a cup of tea and some kooka, and we fixed them up in the cook house.

The young man then asked me if I would go and tow their car back to camp to see if they could fix it. "No problem, you can come with me in the grader and show me where it is." We turned off the road near the camp and headed north across a flat area, then we came to a massive pebble half buried in large sandy bank. We followed a track up towards the centre of the stone. It was about fifty feet long. Twenty feet of it was sticking out of the ground but there must have been another twenty feet below ground level. To its centre was a vertical crack almost three feet wide. "Look down there" the young man said. Leaning forward I could see that the bottom half was filled with clear water. I was amazed to think that you could die of thirst a few feet away and not know water was there.

We got the Holden back to camp but there was nothing we could do without a new radiator hose. Mimili was twenty five kilometres away. The only transport I had in camp was the tipper truck, and the unmade part of the road was soft sand. So at midnight I set off knowing I might well get bogged down. It was so bad I could only get into seventh gear on the twelve speed box. The young man promised to see the doctor in the morning and get some of his mates to get a new hose and collect his car from camp.

It was men's business (ritual) on 8th November with no-one working. I was stuck in camp on my own and had only nine inches of water in the tea urn in the cook house. I wasn't able to go to Mimili to get water, therefore the nine inches would have to last me for the next three days until the ritual was over and the road was opened. Teddy came to camp but he had no water in his long range tank.

That evening we were talking by the camp fire when a scorpion about five inches long paid us a visit. It was moving pretty fast so I jumped onto my chair to get out of its path. Ted shone a torch on it and it froze, then he put a stick under its tail and lifted it sideways. I took my cup back to my van and when I returned it was still there, rigid. We left it where it was, alive, and went our separate ways to bed. Ted told me that when he was young he used to play with them, knowing full well they could give a nasty sting or even kill with their tails.

One day I had to collect our 12e 17g grader from Hastings Dearing the Caterpillar dealers in Alice using our low loader. The only trouble was there was no registration on it due to the fact that it wasn't required on the homeland and the permit had run out. Deb made an arrangement with Caterpillar to use their trade plates for the six hour trip back to camp and return them by coach the next day.

We couldn't stop on our journey down the Stuart highway in case we were spotted, so I picked up my mate Harry in Alice and we began our trip south, stopping occasionally to check the chains securing the grader to the low loader. We were nearly two hours into our trip, about twenty minutes short of Earldunda when I began to get terrible cramping pains in my stomach.

Once more I got out to check the load, and as I walked around the back of the low loader my vision became blurred. I pitched head first down a twelve foot gravel embankment. I could feel gravel in between my teeth and my lips. Then suddenly the pain stopped - everything was quiet.

Coming towards me was a slim woman dressed in a short sleeved white silky looking blouse with two shoulder bands going over her shoulders and a pleated skirt. She had what looked like short blonde hair. Her left hand was down by her side while her right arm was upright and she was waving a white handkerchief as though trying to attract my attention. I thought 'How beautiful, I wonder who she is.' There was no skyline, no ground, everything had a pale blue background. Either I was moving towards her or she was moving towards me. She seemed to glide very slowly closer. I was waiting for her to get near enough for me to see her features in more detail.

Suddenly I was wide awake yelling my head off. Harry had been watching me when I plunged down the embankment, and he'd dragged me back up and propped me in the shade of the truck. Slowly my vision came back but my breathing was in short sharp spasms. "Can you sit up?" I was asked. "Yes I think so." I didn't recognise the voice. Turned out Tony (watti warra) had been passing on his way to the homeland and witnessed everything. "Geez Bob I thought you were a goner, you turned blue. Can Harry drive the truck?" "Yes." "Then you can come with me, Earldunda is just a few minutes up the road."

Once there I wobbled into the kitchen. Greg took one look at me. "Strewth what's happened to you Robbie?" I told him over two mugs of hot milk. "Better phone Deb and tell her what's happened." She sounded worried. "You and Harry stay there the night and you can come back to Alice and get checked out at the hospital tomorrow."

My ribs and shoulder were killing me and I had very little sleep that night, but worst of all was Harry's snoring! If he hadn't been with me that day I would almost certainly have died of heat stroke. He saved my life. The next day he went on his way to camp with the low loader and I managed to get a lift into Alice with a rep. The hospital x-rays revealed bruised ribs and right shoulder and the nurse told me it would take longer to heal than a fracture due to the fact that the bruising was over a large area.

The doctor gave me a sick note and that was that. I made my way over to Deb's office and gave her the news.

"Robbie I don't want you driving for a few days. When you get to camp the mechanic can pick up Colin on the cook's run. I've booked you in at the Desert Rose for the night and you can catch the coach for Indulkana tomorrow. I'd like you to remain in camp and take it easy for a day or two, then contact me when you feel better." How was I going to remain in camp doing nothing? Luckily the men were now capable of operating all the plant in a safe and efficient way. Ted was running the road gang without my help, sorting out the wages, and really coming good. The men were happy.

Soon it was time for the four days rest period and I would have some peace in camp on my own, or so I thought. Tommy had other ideas. Once again, as though by some pre-arranged signal, after I switched off the generator set I saw two lots of headlights heading for his camp.

I sensed there was something wrong due to the children crying. I was told later by Colin the reason was that the strangers would be putting on war paint. Tommy had recruited the services of a fierce witchdoctor and his mob in an attempt to drive me out. Once again I made my way with my swag quietly to the cook house and waited. Everything was quiet, then I heard what sounded like river stones clanking together near my van.

Suddenly the stones were hitting my van both front and back, accompanied by short shrill whistles. Then silence. It was obvious they were listening at my van for any movements. The next thing they did was to move in groups, tapping each van with a stick.

First one light tap, then another, then another, each at about three second intervals. Then silence. After about a minute they would do it again, each time getting louder and louder, until they were banging really hard. I could see the shadows of the men as they passed the camp fire. At around three thirty they found me. I heard them rubbing against the pipe and the gas bottle. I was unarmed, what could I do? Okay may as well bluff it out. Holding my dolphin torch without switching it on, I rubbed it along the rough sand-covered floor. It broke the silence with a weird grinding sound. 'Okay mister gudarchi man, you've found me, come on inside, I've got something for you, but I don't think you'll like it.'

I watched the dying flames of the camp fire reflecting on the open door of the cook house. 'What's going to happen now they've found me, will they rush the cook house or maybe wait until I appear outside?'

I kept playing over in my mind the sound of stones hitting my van. Time for some quick thinking, got to arm myself. I switched on my torch and walked to Colin's drawer beneath the service counter and took out a large carving knife and a sharpening steel. I pushed them into the ruler pocket of my cut-down overalls. I waited and waited. Tommy's dog barked as though welcoming someone.

Nothing for it but to get out of the cook house. Walking to the edge of the camp I started up the generator set. The lights on the bottom of the vans gave me some reassurance. No shadows, no people, just sand and scrub.

Walking back to the camp fire I threw on a pile of wood, then taking my swag from the cook house I spread it out by the welcoming fire. All that time sitting still in the cook house had left me feeling chilled. Deliberately I went and switched off the generator set and got into my swag. By now the fire was going well and I was warm and comfortable. I felt myself nodding off, only to be awakened by the sound of a single vehicle heading away from Tommy's camp. Once again I fell asleep. At first light I went into the cook house and made myself a cup of tea. Taking it back to my van I sat on the top step, grateful for the peace and quiet.

After a couple of minutes I caught a glance of someone moving stealthily between the vans and heading my way. He obviously didn't notice me sitting there. As he drew near I asked him calmly "Do you want something?" I had caught him completely by surprise. He was tall and slim, around six feet tall, late forties early fifties, with wild grey hair and big brown staring eyes. He was dressed in a shirt and blue jeans. It took him a few seconds to gain his composure. "I want a puncture outfit." I was comfortable with the fact that he seemed wrong-footed by my calm appearance. I knew he was the fierce witchdoctor set on me by Tommy and I was relieved it didn't come to a fight because I would have been killed, but I would have done my best to take a couple of them with me.

"Okay I'll get you one out of the container on one of the trailers. Funny thing, I felt no animosity towards him - on the contrary I had a sneaking admiration for him. As I stepped up onto the trailer tow bar I noticed his eyes widen. He'd spotted the knife and sharpening steel protruding from my ruler pocket - he couldn't keep his eyes off them.

Probing in the container I found a tin box containing patches, glue, chalk and a small rough file. "Here you are, but I want them back when you've finished with them." I stared into his eyes and he stared into mine. I held the tin for a few seconds before releasing it.

'I don't suppose I'll see this kit again' I thought to myself - and I didn't. I watched him walk up the hill out of sight towards Tommy's humpy. A short while later the other vehicle drove away from his camp. Later that afternoon Peter drove into camp looking really worried. "Robbie you got trouble?" "No Pete, I'm okay." He must have heard a rumour back in Indulkana, but there was no way I was going to involve the men in my problems, after all my job was to keep them together.

There was a very bad sand storm that night and as usual I went to the cook house and made myself a cup of tea at about one o'clock. I was still tense from the previous night's experience. Everything was rocking and shaking but I eventually got to sleep. By morning the storm had blown itself out, but after a short inspection around the camp I discovered the ablutions van had been blown off its stabilisers. At that time I was the only one in camp. I lifted it back to its original position with the Hough front-end loader which caused my ribs and shoulder to be very sore. I was very limited in my movements but it didn't stop me from cooking myself a decent mid-day meal.

The following night was still and beautiful but there were lots of mosquitoes around. After I'd taken a shower I decided to sleep outside but they drove me mad, so I went back into my van and dropped a mosquito net over my bed. By leaving the door open I had a lovely night's sleep. The men were back the next day, and we moved all our gear to camp six.

Teddy was really coming good as the supervisor. He was starting to make decisions and sticking by them. He knew what conditions he wanted his men to work to. Two hundred kilometres for the next twelve months - 1986 - was I felt attainable. Deb knew her job well, and to her credit had come through a lot of hard decision making. She was totally different from the giggly immature girl I first met twelve months previous. It was always quite obvious that she had the aptitude and ability to assume the responsibilities put upon her.

I couldn't get Ted to use that bloody diary of his, but I kept on to him about it. Also I told him to think positively in his approach to his employment i.e. the position of supervisor was a step up, not a step down - and to not even consider getting a job as a machine operator with another contractor making the sealed part of the Stuart highway. I'm glad to say he listened to me - that was all I wanted.

In November all the men, including Tommy were working well. Sandy cut one kilometre of new road with the 12e 17g Cat. grader. Tommy was cutting a new line with the D6 dozer just to the east of Mimili gate.

Albert was operating the Cat. 16 heavy grader on the road by Mimili gate, and the rest of the men were moving manta (rock) with the front-end loader and the tip truck. One man was taking fuel out to the machines and the remainder were in camp cleaning up the area. There was no doubt about it they were all working as a team, and all my hard work had been worth it. Soon I would be leaving to head home. The arrangement with the pay master at TAFE was that any time worked as overtime would be taken off my leaving date - thus my date had been brought forward to 8th December.

It would be hard to leave the men. They had educated me and made sure I came to no harm. I was part of a big family with a culture that had helped them survive over thousands of years in a totally hostile environment.

Colin and I went to Mimili to check on the airstrip landing ground. While we were there a light aircraft came in to land. As it touched down there was a southerly wind, but the wind sock was showing a south westerly direction. I mentioned this to the pilot and he said "Yes, the wind sock pole isn't high enough, it's only fifteen feet and is giving a false reading. It needs to be at least thirty to forty feet up due to the small trees around the airfield."

In Mimili we saw the young watti who had come into camp with a scald to his arm and shoulder. "Look" he said with a big grin, and showed us the dressings which Colin had fixed up for him. "Palya" - he was happy.

Later that day Teddy took me to a large water storage tank just outside Mimili, and showed me how to have a shower with a half-inch hose about fifteen feet long. "Just throw it over the side and siphon it out." With that he tied a brick to one end to hold the pipe down and threw it into the tank. He told me that if you were to jump into tanks when they were old the sides would sometimes burst and that could be disastrous.

The day had been warm, approximately thirty three degrees, with no wind. Again I tried to sleep outside but had to go back into my van because of the mosquitoes. I dropped the net over my bed and had a good night's sleep.

It was mid-November and I was alone in camp one day. Harry turned up at around twelve o'clock and asked if I had any kooka. I gave him some meat and bread and he took some cold water in a container. Just before he left he said he would call and see me that evening. He came at eight o'clock with kunga number three. She was tall and slim, in about the same age group as Harry - he was thirty two. He gave me two presents (good luck gifts.) Being taken by surprise all I could give him was my cowboy hat and some meat to take with them.

They were driving to Kulka which would take two and a half days. He spoke more to me that night than ever. "Robbie I'll miss you - you're a good friend." "Thanks Harry I'll miss you too. I might come and visit you one day and bring my wife with me." He took my hand in his and looked down at me. He was almost crying - it was the first time I had ever seen him look unhappy, and I felt like crying too. Trying to compose myself I asked him if he wanted some ice cream. "Owa." "Okay I've got some in the freezer." They stayed for about an hour then went on their way. It seemed like something and someone important had just slipped out of my life and I couldn't do anything about it.

The fuel delivery truck and trailer arrived at nine thirty. The driver stayed over and slept in his cab. I slept in my van and got bitten by mosquitoes because I forgot to drop the net over my bed. The next night I had a good sleep in the cook house with its air conditioning. I was awake at about seven o'clock and by ten the sun was beginning to break through. The clouds were lifting but it was still cool. I sat by my van filling in a report sheet and my diary, but had to move into the shade as the sun was too bright on the pages, causing me to have double vision.

I cooked a nice mid-day meal for myself washed down with black tea. Just before six o'clock Willie, a young friend of mine, and two of his anangu mates came into camp and begged six point 22 bullets off me. They were going to shoot malu (kangaroo.) At seven o'clock they returned, knocking on the cook house door. "Palya Willie?" "Owa." "Did you get any malu?" "Wia" (no.)

He asked me if I had any engine oil. "Yes I'll go and get you some." I found a container in the back of the white Toyota and filled it from our stock tank in the workshop trailer. "Here you are Willie." As I handed it to him he asked in a whisper "Have you got any kooka?" It was a rule that anyone coming into camp not employed by AP Roads must not be given food, otherwise we wouldn't get rid of them and the men's rations and mine would suffer. With water it was a different matter, that was never refused.

"Wia Willie, if cookie found out he would cut my throat." I made a gesture drawing my hand across my throat. "I thought you anangu were supposed to be great hunters." He shook his head. "Tell you what - how does a jam sandwich and a cup of tea sound?" "Owa." He began to laugh. "Palya Robbie."

We ran out of water the next day and I had to collect some from Mimili in the long range tank in the back of my Toyota. Colin came into camp at eight thirty in the evening and I steered him to bed. At ten twenty five he made his way to the cook house, but decided to turn round and go back. He got down the steps okay but fell flat out on the sand and still kept up the walking motion.

The following day I went to Fregon to see the next section of road they would be constructing. The new guy operating the Caterpillar 16 was coming along fine until he spiked one of the tyres on a mulgar root. He was so upset he ran away, but I told Ted not to be too hard on him, after all it could happen to anyone. A short while later he came back and everything was forgotten.

Since the last run- in with the fierce witchdoctor and his crew they had left me alone, and I was able to give the men my full attention. Everyone was working in a safe and professional manner and they didn't need me anymore, but it would be hard to say goodbye on the eighth of December.

The Australian from TAFE who should have kept in monthly contact with me had retired some time ago and a young aboriginal guy had taken over his job as senior lecturer. He was new at the job and had a tendency to talk down to me which I didn't like, so we never really hit it off. He was at the meeting when I was advised by Colin not to let Billy come back because of fears for his safety. I couldn't tell him or Deb the reason for that for fear of losing the men on the road gang. Maybe he resented me for that. He did come past once every month but he never called in to see me at the camp or when I was working on the road with the men. That was until one hot day at the end of November.

I saw a dust trail approaching from the east and was surprised when he pulled up in his air conditioned jeep. He didn't offer to get out, instead he spoke to me through the open window of the driver's door. I thought 'At last he's come to collect all my written daily and weekly reports' but no such luck. "Hello, do you want a cup of tea?" I expected him to get out and go into the cook house but he ignored my question.

"I've been told the men don't want you here, and I want you to go immediately." I couldn't believe my ears. "Why, what's wrong?" "You must go, I want you out of here." "But what about the road programme, and my reports?" "I don't want them, and as far as I'm concerned it's been a complete failure." "Surely you want my reports for the last twelve months." "No, the men want you out of here, you must go."

For once I was speechless. He closed his window and drove off back in the direction from whence he came, to the east and Indulkana. I felt as though someone had hit me with a pole axe. As if in a dream I walked over to my van, took a last look at the pile of paperwork on the shelf, picked everything up, and made my way up a nearby hill. I looked out across the desert valley that had been my home for almost a year, and held the papers out flat on my hands as though making some sort of ancient sacrifice. Slowly the papers began to drift away from me one by one.

Some were damp with the tears I was shedding. Still in a dream I returned to camp to await the arrival of the men for their evening meal.

With all my overtime allowance I was due to leave camp on eighth of December, but this now meant I would have to leave on the fourth. Nothing for it but to radio Deb and give her the news. She was surprised and sounded upset when I told her what had happened, never-the-less she accepted it and booked me a ticket with the Greyhound coach service for the fourth.

Soon the men would be returning for their tea, so all I had to do was wait. After the last man had entered the cook house it was time to face them and get to the bottom of the situation. I entered the cook house expecting hostility, but instead they greeted me in their usual way "Palya Robbie." At this point I was bewildered as to why they wanted me out. After explaining to them what had transpired between myself and the TAFE guy they were as baffled as I was. Then the penny dropped.

Apparently the men had been working near Mimili gate to the west of the camp. The direction that the TAFE guy had come from and returned to was the east (Indulkana) - and Tommy had returned there when he jacked it in a couple of days earlier. Someone said he left because he had too many enemies in Mimili and he wasn't popular there. So that was it! Tommy was at the bottom of all this and not the men.

Then I remembered what uncle Leslie had said - always talk to the snake's head, not it's tail. I knew what I had to do.

On my way back home for the final time I decided to call in at TAFE in

Adelaide. The Director General was away, so I asked his secretary if I could leave him a note. "No problem." In it I described the manner in which I had been treated by the so-called Senior Lecturer. It was thorough and I spared no detail, listing everything that had transpired in the last twelve months. Being satisfied, I continued on my journey to Melbourne and my Cathie.

Early in 1986 I received a reference from the Director General of TAFE Adelaide, and in the final part he stated: "The area in which Mr. Westworth was teaching is very remote, only accessible easily by air. The climate is very hot and arid for much of the year. His task of living in the aboriginal community and teaching the young men was extremely daunting, never-the-less he sustained great enthusiasm for the work and saw the project through to its successful conclusion. At the end of his contract he had trained ten young men to confidently operate the equipment and construct excellent roads in the North West lands."

It turned out that he had read my note and the guy who betrayed me was called to his office, given a bollocking, and was also threatened with the sack. Deb also sent me an excellent reference. The matter had been cleared up and I was happy, remembering what uncle told me - "Always talk to the snake's head."

It was now time for me to leave Alice Springs for the last time and head for Cooberpede along the four hundred and fifty kilometres of unmade highway, calling in at Woomera where a large concrete water tank tilted like a drunken sailor. This was due to the security guards digging for opal under the tank in their spare time. Then on to Port Pirrie and Port Augusta before arriving in Adelaide.

On that day all the men in the road gang bought me gifts. Boomerangs, music sticks and lizards.

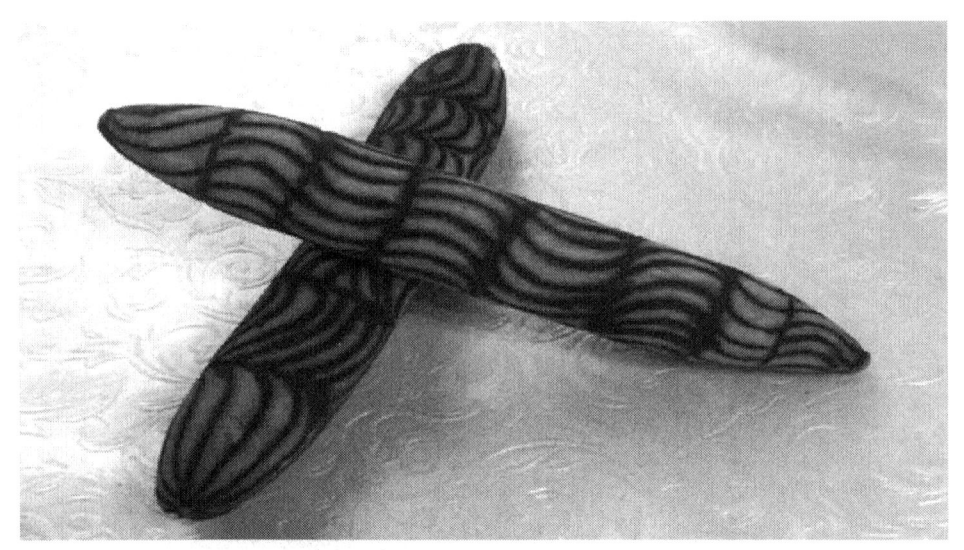

The ladies who had danced for me presented me with a necklace made with seeds and two fruit gathering dishes.

All of these gifts were made especially for me. I was happy and sad. Happy that all the gifts were good luck gifts, and sad because I was leaving all these wonderful people who had treated me as one of their own.

I was especially sad that the man who had adopted me and cared for me wasn't there. Leslie, the chief tribal dancer for mens business. He treated me as though I was his own son, even putting his life on the line when I was faced by a man wielding a nulla nulla.

For the last time I stuffed all my belongings into my overnight bag. I tidied up my bed with its warm blankets for whoever wanted it, and made sure my van was tidy, then Sandy took me into Indulkana to catch the Greyhound coach.

When we reached Mimili gate I took one last look around and was pleased that the men, against all odds, had completed seventy kilometres of new road. I say against all odds because some of them had never worked to strict hours and most of them had never driven mobile equipment before. No-one was injured or had any accidents. It was as though they had a sixth sense regarding safety.

The coach was there when we reached Indulkana. I took one last look at the medical centre where the witch doctor had saved me from chemical poisoning, and I said goodbye to the guy in charge of the local garage workshop. He was also the Indulkana grader driver. Then I boarded the coach.

We stopped at Marla Bore for a brief period, and before we drove away I took a last look at the two transport containers which served as the cop shop and looked across the sandy road at the back track to Indulkana. Suddenly the reality of leaving kicked in and I felt desperately sad. As we left Marla Bore I also took one last look at the hotel motel with its long low front veranda. I remembered the young Jillaroos I had met there as they worked their way up to Darwin from Adelaide.

They were young, pretty, and talkative. "We don't get much money but the boss buys us cowboy boots, jeans and denim jackets. When we feel like it we move on to the next job getting closer to Darwin, and we'll take any job going, even bar work." Jillaroos do the same jobs as Jackeroos on big homesteads mustering cattle and so on, but the boss gets the best end of the deal in cheap labour.

The journey to Adelaide from Alice, allowing for all the twists and turns in the old road at that time, was around seventeen hundred kilometres long. Today it's shorter due to the straighter sealed section that has been completed.

When I arrived in Adelaide the first thing I did was to go to the education building in Flinders Street and leave some outstanding paperwork for the Director General of TAFE Adelaide.

Then I rang my friend the exchange teacher. As luck would have it she was at home, and I thanked her for the time she put me up when I was between coaches on my R and R. She was pleased to hear that I was okay and wished me well on my travels. "Don't forget Robbie, any time you're up here call in." "I won't forget, and god bless."

From Alice to Adelaide took twenty hours. This time I didn't have to wait too long for the coach to Melbourne, and seven hours later my beautiful wife met me at the coach station. One and a half hours later we were home in Warburton.

Cathie and I had no intention of relocating to the UK, but in 1986 we decided to take a two months holiday there to catch up on family and friends.

When we arrived we were shocked to see how frail her mother was. We could have put her up in a granny flat back at our house in Warburton but she wouldn't leave her friends and family. It really upset us both.

After almost ten years away everything seemed different. Although we were immigrants in an English speaking country it was hard to see just how much circumstances had changed back in the UK.

'Blood is thicker than water' as the saying goes, so there and then we decided that we would have to relocate to a new life in the UK. We returned to Australia at the end of our holiday, and in March 1987 we said goodbye to our beautiful home in the mountains of Victoria.

Chapter 8
UK calling

With our two Staffordshire Bull Terriers in quarantine we searched for a home in Rugeley, West Midlands. Rugeley was a small mining town in those days, but when the coal mines closed miners were put out of work. Times were hard.

Six months after moving in we were joined by our dogs, Sally and Billy. It must have been somewhat of a shock for them after the freedom of the mountains, but Cannock Chase made up for it. Cathie would take them for walks every morning.

Employment for me was difficult to find. Back in Australia I had been an instructor and examiner on major construction plant. After making enquiries I was told that I could be an examiner here if I took a course and paid £1,000 up front! That was a body blow. Where the hell was I going to get that money from with all my commitments? In Australia I got my ticket on pure ability and experience. Here it seems you have to pay your way in. I was disappointed to say the least - but not to worry, I became a JCB driver which took me all over Birmingham, Aston, the jewellery quarter, Erdington, Sutton, and many more places, even as far as Coventry and Rugby. Then I took a job in Lichfield as a tower crane operator for a concrete firm.

After about three years I decided to go self employed, driving rough terrain telescopic handlers in the house building industry, working for major construction companies here in the Midlands.

However I couldn't lose the travel bug, and twice a year I would throw my sleeping bag, tent, and cooking gear into my car and head off to the continent travelling throughout France, Spain, and Italy. Cathie was a home bird, and wasn't interested in holidays - she was always happy at home. We did fly out to southern Italy once on a week's holiday, but she told me that she was happy to be at home so that was that.

One day she asked me to install a drainage system around our house to take the water away from the footings of the front bay, but there was a problem. Before I could dig any trenches or lay any pipes there were gas, electric, phone, and water services below ground and all within the area of excavation. It was then that I remembered something I'd discovered way back before we emigrated to Australia. I discovered that I had the gift and understanding of dowsing. I could detect any sort of pipe, cable, or cavity underground and chart them - no need for any expensive ground radar systems.

I even picked up Roman culverts. Could I still do it after all these years? Time to find out. I fashioned a pair of dowsing rods from some heavy cable which I found in the garage, and began systematically scouring the area between the main road and the house. It worked! After all those years!

The sewer pipes were at the rear of the house so there was no problem with them. That left water, gas, electric and phone. After careful investigation I discovered an extra service intersecting with the drainage line of trench. There were only supposed to be four. Had I lost my touch? Carefully I began to dig. First I found the yellow gas pipe, then I found the electric cable. Okay so far. Next was the blue plastic water pipe, and finally I exposed the phone ducting. That was okay, but what was the fifth reaction on the rods? Was it my imagination? Was there anything there? I again began digging. At first there was nothing, then to my relief I found it. A green plastic pipe. Turned out it was put there in preparation for cable television.

So there you have it - after all those years and at the ripe old age of fifty - I still retained the ability to use dowsing rods.

2008 was a bad year for the construction industry. Work was slowing down, men were losing their jobs, and I was no exception. I was seventy one years old and knew that I would never find work again, and sitting around in the house wasn't an option. What could I do?

Having not long lost my beautiful lurcher (Lady) to old age, I decided to look around for a pup to take her place. I met two people at a dog show in Lichfield who had a skinny little whippet-greyhound cross. He was put into Cathie's arms and that was it. I knew she wouldn't let him go. His coat was short and his colouring was black and white, more like that of a border collie. We named him Badger.

Straight away I would take him for walks with our two staffies tagging along. He was full of beans, and soon I was having to take him on his own. He would run for miles without a break, and at the age of four months he caught his first rabbit. It took me twenty minutes of coaxing to get it from him, but gradually I taught him to let me carry his kill. I'm sure he knew that it would end up in the pot for himself and the staffies. He was like lightening, and could cover four points of the compass in a flash.

Then in a matter of weeks I realized that he wouldn't respond to a whistle, but instead he would work on hand signals. Point to the left and he would go left. Point to the right and he would go right. Make a sweeping motion with my arm and he would head out in a circle. Beckon him back with my arm and he would come back. Show him the flat of my hand and he would stop.

I realized that I'd been blessed with a remarkable dog, and this was great because we could work together without any whistles or shouting, so no-one would know we were there.

Night-time working was out, there were too many obstacles. I didn't want Badger injured with any bits of farm machinery left lying around. Two farmers gave us permission to work their fields, and very soon he became stock trained.

He was no problem with livestock, poultry or farmyard cats. One of the farmers even asked us to watch his stock and house for a week, usually twice a year, while he and his wife went on holiday.

Badger would take himself off at three in the morning and return a short while later, usually with a rabbit which we shared in the pot. I always made sure there were no farm implements left out in the fields or under hedgerows for him to get injured on.

There was a problem with foxes killing geese on one of the farms. Some were found with their heads and necks bitten off. After a bit of tracking Badger saw three of them off.

Grey squirrels, rabbits and bigger stuff were often on his list of kills, and the freezer was full of them on numerous occasions. Summer sun or winter snow made no difference to Badger, the result was always the same.

I took him to a couple of country shows - not as an entrant - just for a break. They had working gun dogs retrieving small dummies. He watched them work and I knew what he was thinking - 'I can do that.'

At the sheep dog trials he used to get really excited and twitchy as he watched them working. Even now when it's on television he reacts in just the same way.

Whilst at the shows he was always calm, even when the guns were being fired at the clay pigeons. People would notice him and quite often someone would comment and ask me if he was for sale. My reply was always the same. "There's not enough money in the bank to buy him."

Plus fours, a gillet and a flat cap usually denoted some grumpy old gamekeeper who'd clocked us, and of course they guessed right, because Badger and I had been running rings around the gamekeepers and rangers.

I suppose things have gone full circle now - from my boyhood as a young poacher to the present day. It's a funny old life don't you think?

Chapter 9
Aboriginal Terminology

Anangu - Aboriginal people

Buck - Young man

Cabi Water

Gina - Tracks

Gudarchi man or Feather foot - Bogey man (similar to a hired killer)

Jin - Young female

Jingaroo - Maybe

Kunga - Wide

Malu - Kangaroo

Manta - Rock

Mumble - Ghost

Nula nula - Fighting wooden club

Nyuntu - You

Owa - Yes

Palya - Okay, Good

Pitjanjatjara - Name of the tribe (pronounced as Pitnjara)

Pitjanjatjaraku - People of the Pitjanjatjara

Road a cali cali - Twisting road

Wanambi - Invisible spirit snake (can be as big as a man)

Watti - Man (Wadi)

White manta - White stone (used to fill low spots in road building)

Wia - No

Robert at home in Rugeley 2016

Printed in Great Britain
by Amazon

54713896R00084